CATCHING SIGHT OF GOD

CATCHING SIGHT OF GOD

Discovering the Wonder
of Every Day

CHERYL FORBES

MULTNOMAH · PRESS

Portland, Oregon 97266

Cover design by Lois Kent Davis
Photography by Steve Terrill
Edited by Liz Heaney

CATCHING SIGHT OF GOD
© 1987 by Cheryl Forbes
Published by Multnomah Press
Portland, Oregon 97266

Multnomah Press is a ministry of Multnomah School of the Bible,
8435 NE Glisan Street, Portland, OR 97220

Printed in the United States of America

Library of Congress Cataloging-in-Publication Data

Forbes, Cheryl.
  Catching sight of god.

  1. Meditations.   2. Forbes, Cheryl.
I. Title.
BV4832.2.F622   1987   242   87-12226
ISBN 0-88070-196-X

87 88 89 90 91 92 93 – 10 9 8 7 6 5 4 3 2 1

To Allen Jr. and to Greg

who have taught me more

than they realize

Contents

In the Beginning

W hat follows is a love story—not a novel, but a story nonetheless. I am living this story; so are you, or you could be. Small, everyday events—a cedar chest of remembrances and joys—make up the plot. The people are members of my family—my closest friends— and they are as important to this story as any character in any novel you will read. They are shaping me, changing me, encouraging me, challenging me. Without them, I would not be who I am. As they change, so do I.

A good storyteller lets the reader know each of his characters by the others in his tale. Their interaction propels the plot forward, just as much as do the circumstances of this story. God is a good storyteller. He works through the characters in my life just as much as he works through the circumstances. You may not have the same context I do; for example, you may live where there are only two seasons. But you have characters in your life as funny, as unusual, and as sometimes maddening as I do. When you look at the people I know, I want you to see those you hold dear. If you do it as if for the first time, I will have succeeded.

Here, then, is my cast of characters. Although some will appear more frequently than others, they are all important:

Allen Sr.—my husband, mathematician, classic guitarist, singer, writer.

Allen Jr.—my elder son, a budding musician and jazz guitarist, well on his way to becoming a person.

Greg—my younger son, a fishing and riding fanatic and lover of baseball; he helps keep me on top of the game.

My mother—another lover of baseball—a Cubs fan from way back, and lover of all animals, large and small, horses in particular.

My brother, Steven, who is Steve to everyone but me, a musician and lover of fantasy; he shares my enthusiasm for cooking.

Stephanie, my first sister, also a writer, the closest to me in age and once closest to me in interests; though we both still love to read and garden, she can't understand how fishing appeals to me.

Although there are other characters in my life—father, another sister, grandparents—these are the ones who appear most frequently, often in the past rather than in the present. They may be different people now from those I remember.

1 A Sorbet for the Senses, A Sight for Sore Eyes

However much we like to think of ourselves as rational creatures—and we are, to a degree—what reaches us most is not the rational argument, the bald equation, or the cut-and-dried language of lawyers; rather, it is artistry.

Artists appear everywhere. You may have one living near you whose work with a tomato surpasses Burpee's. Perhaps your neighbor has a knack of flower arranging that the editors of *Horticulture* magazine would envy or a sense of perennial landscaping that rivals that of Gertrude Jekyll. In the kitchen, Julia Child may have no advantage over your father. And as for painting, what's Grandma Moses compared to your mother's work with water colors and acrylics?

But perhaps we've failed to notice everyday artistry. Maybe too many Micky D's or too much color TV have jaded our palates. God, the consummate artist, cannot reach us, and soon all we see is that once-a-year fiery sunset or the screaming sunrise that demands lie-a-beds to the floor. We are in need of a sorbet for the senses, tangy, chillingly clear.

Most of us have a love-hate relationship with the senses; yet Scripture glories in them. Why else would death be the archenemy; why else would the promise of a new earth recur throughout the Bible? God's promises and blessings come to us through our senses. Our story—this story God is writing, this story I am telling— takes place on earth, the dusty side of his kingdom, the side he will one day return to its original polish. That's why, too, certain events in our lives seem unrelated to us, though not to God. He uses many kinds of language, different styles of writing to tell the same story, just as he did in Scripture, just as Jesus did in his parables.

If God sends us his blessings through the senses, why do we ignore them? When was the last time we noticed the texture of the wool V-neck sweater we donned in the morning? Or the silk tie we chose to wear with it? How long has it been since the scent of simmering soup excited us or the feel of freshly whipped cream amazed us? We're afraid that to enjoy the senses is somehow unchristian, hedonistic. It is only hedonism when we worship the senses themselves. If we delight in the senses as gifts from God, which they are, then it is worship of quite another kind. This worship is continuous, daily, nonstop—a romping riot of thankfulness.

Our ability to worship depends on our angle of vision. A mouse scampers across the floor. Do we see vermin, or can we see, with Walt Whitman, "a miracle"? Is the crabgrass that grows through the sidewalk a gardening nuisance, or is it reassurance of the irrepressible power of life?

Wouldn't God's view be positive rather than negative? And shouldn't we share his view? This earthly kingdom is our inheritance: to hate, fear, mistrust, or ignore it is to trample our most important possession.

Although it takes some practice, we can acquire the habit of looking at life from God's view—with all its rich possibilities—rather than from our own narrow, negative shortsightedness.

In retrospect we can easily understand that life has a rhythm drummed by God, a pattern and a shape cut by him. But we need to know that in the present. In the odd moments of our lives we should recognize God tantalizing us with clues about his purposes and his character. Life's major issues—career, marriage, family—may not be as important as the minor ones. Jesus talks about small things—a lost coin, a seed in the ground, two sparrows. Have I cared for them? Did I clean the corners, or just the large space in the middle of the floor? When I made my last fire, did I first pile large log on large log, or did I start with newspaper, small kindling, larger kindling, a few small thorn apple limbs, and then, only when the fire was going well, add a big chunk of black walnut? When I read Jesus' words about the small things, I recall the Old Testament story of Elijah. God was not in the big things—the wind, the fire, the storms; he was a still, small voice. God speaks, but can we hear him? Is his voice too quiet for us? Is our own voice too loud?

What does God have to do with eggs and bacon, the odd bowl of oatmeal eaten on the run, or our quarrels about who feeds the cat or empties the trash? Why would he be around when the refrigerator needs to be cleaned or the car washed? (*We* wouldn't, if we could help it.) These are the boring but necessary details of life. Yet, even if we hire someone else to remove the onion skins from the bottom of the refrigerator or to take our car to the local brushless car wash, we're still involved with the activity. It's unhealthy to avoid the routines of life— saving our energies for the momentous or at least the entertaining. Life can't be one trip after another to

Wrigley Field, with the home team winning in the bottom of the ninth. And who would want it to be? Avoiding the ordinary only makes the extraordinary meaningless—and it distorts reality.

We want life to be a neat package tied with a pretty bow. Everything must make sense, all the transitions obvious. We like our people that way too. We would prefer everyone to be predictable characters in a potboiler—the villain, the innocent beauty, the hero. Because we don't like loose ends, unresolved issues, unexplained events, or contrary families, we beg God to let us write the story—or at least read ahead. Just once we'd like to skip from chapter three to chapter eleven. But that's not the kind of reading God wants us to do. We've got to take the plot as it unfolds, with all its unexpected and unexplained twists and turns. God wants us to make the connections between the seemingly unconnected events and people in our lives. What *do* baseball and the Resurrection have to do with one another? Little things first, then the big ones: minor league baseball before the majors, scrambled eggs before an omelet.

I've got lots of scrambled eggs in my life. You probably do too. But do you know the how, the when, and the where of them? Are they creamy or runny—or just dried out? Do they need a little salt and pepper, or are they seasoned with minced onion and green pepper? Is it whole grain toast with a homemade crunch, or english muffins oozing with butter? A late night snack or an early morning send-off for excited fly fishermen? How and when and where do you like your life?

W e have so much to see and know, yet so little time in which to do it. And if our lack of time isn't enough to convince us to widen our sights, what about that old truism, "There's more to life than meets the eye"—certainly true of baseball, breakfasts, and people; it's even true of ourselves. We eye the mirror each morning and think, *That's me. Well, sort of* . . . We sense there's more—much more—to us, even more than our thoughts or feelings. Indeed, there is.

For example, we are a universe within a universe. Right now we have several lives existing simultaneously within us. Our cells have a microlife without which our macrolife would be impossible. Each *cell* has its own mitochondria, and each mitochondrion has its own simple DNA. Mitochondria have one purpose: to produce energy. Without our mitochondria doing what they should, we couldn't do what we should—work, pray, love our neighbor, care for our spouse, worship God: We would die. Our bodies are intricate interrelationships, each part performing a function necessary to the other parts. Mitochondria may be hidden from our sight, but we can be thankful they know their business.

Of course, we may not know a thing about mitochondria, but we know that if we don't eat, we won't live. For most of us, once the chicken goes from the fork to the taste buds, down the esophagus and on into the stomach, we're not much concerned— until the next time we smell the succulent aroma of a roasting hen. But our mitochondria know. The mitochondria and their universe, the cell, are in symbiotic relationship with each other (and with the rest of us, as well, only not so directly). Because the cell provides some protein the mitochondria need to grow and reproduce, and that reproduction assures that the cell will in turn have enough energy to grow and divide, we can reach over each morning to turn off the alarm, get up, take a shower, eat breakfast, kiss our spouse farewell, and head off for a good day's work. (Maybe if you aren't energetic enough in the morning, you need to have a quiet talk with your mitochondria.)

God has seen to it through our mothers—all mitochondria come from our maternal side—that we've got the energy for life. Whether we think of mitochondria in the microworld or of those people who serve as mitochondria in the macroworld, we see that we dependent creatures are too often unaware of our own dependence. Of course we can't spend hours contemplating mitochondria, but we can occasionally give them a thought or give God a word of praise for creating such creatures within us. If God had left it to us, we'd never get that protein metabolized or those cells split; we'd always run a little behind schedule.

For the mitochondria in our macroworld, however, we can and should give a great deal of thought. Each of us has people who are metaphoric mitochondria. They give us the zip, the energy, the extra push we need. I am my husband's mitochondria in the morning; he is certainly mine in the evening. I get him up on time, choose clothes that more or less match, and fix him the kind of breakfast his body needs in the morning—big. At night he keeps me entertained enough so that I can stay awake through dinner, then he does the dishes and lets me read. He gives me physical and spiritual energy. Throughout the day we exchange our roles regularly. We do this automatically, unswervingly, unerringly—or almost. At various times, other people serve as my mitochondria.

Taking a rest from this world to look at another, even if the other world is within myself, always refreshes me. The light hits my eyes in a different way when I've been using them elsewhere. After living in Fangorn's forest for a while—Tolkien's world—the trees surrounding my house look more intense, more treeish. As I weed a flower bed I wait for one of them to walk over and greet me. It hasn't happened yet—but it will. My eyes frequently need a good wash in some light other than my own. I'm glad that God knows this, too, and provides mitochondria and Tolkien and my husband and children and parents and friends to enlighten my eyes.

B ut how do I really see? With my eyes or with God's grace? As the discoverers of optics learned, the eye doesn't really *see* anything. The important part is played by light. Our eyes simply record the light that strikes our retinas.

Because God knows that our eyes are too light sensitive to survive the intensity of his face, he sends us little lights, mere hints and snatches, different angles and prisms of himself. God shows me his face when my husband thanks me for a meal. God shows me his face when he sends a friend to correct my attitude. God shows me his face when my mother gently—or not-so-gently—chides but still loves me. His light comes unexpectedly, unannounced. Sometimes, we must confess, we'd rather have darkness. We might accept a three-point sermon on Sunday, but why must he hide a simple point—or four—in a shadow that stretches across the living room carpet when it is most inconvenient for us to watch? Yet, God wants us prepared for a visit any time he decides to drop in.

When I was young, my mother read me a story about a boy who could never find things, even when they were right under his nose. She liked that story—much better than I did. Every time she'd had a particularly trying day with me she'd read me this story. "Don't you ever look?" she'd scold me, when she had to stop what she was doing to find my socks or shoes or book or dolls or whatever children lose. The boy in the story could sit on top of whatever he was supposed to find and complain that he just couldn't see it, no matter how hard he tried. I often imagine God reading me that story. I hear him say, in my mother's exasperated voice, "Don't you *ever* look?"

We don't look for him on Opening Day. We don't look for him at breakfast or during a business meeting or while changing the baby's diapers—not much there but a soggy bottom. God is sending the light, but our eyes are fractured; our lenses don't fit. Fortunately, however, our eyes are not beyond repair.

God's light and shadow, his back parts and his side views, contain healing properties. Just a glimpse, or a hint of a glimpse, can clear our eyes so that the next time the glimpse or hint of a glimpse is a little clearer, a little stronger, a little longer. Each glance builds on the one before. After a lifetime of seeing, we're ready for a stronger view; we're ready for death. God's light—his grace—sparkles with joy and wonder; it shimmers with commitment, surrender, and sacrifice. It moves from the longest blue day of summer to the shortest gray hours of winter, from the spring of resurrection to the fall of advent. God's grace surrounds and envelops us; we cannot see without it.

People would have us believe that God and his grace operate in the miraculous, the outside-of-nature, so that's what we look for. But what is a miracle? A sudden, unexpected healing? A large windfall? Yes, we'd probably agree that such things are miraculous. But what about the coming of spring? Is that miraculous? Or is it merely ordinary because it happens every year. What about the first snowfall? A beautifully written story? A clean house? A job well done at the office? A superb meal? Although none is extraordinary, each has about it the miraculous. Does anyone ever think *Oh, how boring. Another spring. New flowers. Fresh scents. What a drag.*

We've got a skewed notion of the miraculous. We don't think it comes in anything so simple as reading a good book or eating the first bite of spring asparagus. A tonsillectomy one day, a wedding the next—what do they have to do with one another, we wonder—a visit from an in-law, shopping for groceries, preparing meals, teaching children how to care for themselves, up at 5:30 or 6:00, in bed by 9:00—those are my miracles. Those ordinary events, whatever they might be, spell life; by them I know I am. By them I know that against astronomical odds, I was born: God has said, "Let Cheryl Forbes exist." And by them God comes to me.

In some ways life would be easier if God saved himself for the big moments—the drum roll, the trumpet call, the parted brocade. Then we'd have no doubts, and he'd have our undivided attention. But who wants to give him attention if it means jumping from the table to do the dishes or rake the leaves? If only God would work the way we want him to—but he refuses. We know one thing, though: He's not playing hide and seek with us. That's our game, not his. He's around, just waiting for a call.

He's around when the trout are jumping on the first day of the season. He's around when the house needs to be cleaned or the phone needs to be answered or the oil changed in the crankcase of my car. God's around in every season, lounging on the corner, waiting to be noticed. He's under that rotting stack of leaves; he's peeking up through the hard ground in the first green whiff of the crocus or the last leaf to fall from the maple. Look at him waving his arms, just waiting to be called on; he knows the answers.

2   November Dying

M y father-in-law died in November. I didn't know know him well; he didn't me, either. I belong to a different world than he did, a world in which he felt uncomfortable, unsure of the rules. He wanted a world where independence was still possible, where a person performed for himself nearly every function necessary for life—from building a house to keeping it running. He was not made for the age of experts; he was a jack-of-all-trades. He died an independent death, a November death.

Bill loved flowers, lilacs particularly. He was an amateur horticulturalist, almost the only area left where amateurs can still outdo the professionals (he liked that; he was a professional amateur). Yet, he didn't like cut flowers. He felt they were an impractical extravagance; they died and would never return. Dying and impermanence bothered him more than it bothers most people. He was angry at his disease and angry that this new world held no place for someone of his interests and disposition. He was angry at November. Yet, that's when he died, almost as soon as October yielded itself.

Emily Dickinson would have understood my father-in-law. She isolated herself in Amherst from a world she didn't trust; Bill settled for a mountain in New York. Her attitude toward death? "Because I could not stop for death, he kindly stopped for me," she wrote. It's a poem for November, the month for dying. Under gray skies we see dead leaves, dead flowers, dead vines.

Dickinson wrote, "because I *could* not stop for death"—a verb that affects everything. There's a difference between *will not* and *could not*. We're too busy, she says, too taken up by work and cares to spend the time to die. Death inconveniences us when it disrupts life. It dusts things up, just when we've finished polishing. As with my father-in-law, most of us don't want to rest along the way of our lives, much less stop for death. Death is ugly.

But not for Dickinson: "He kindly stopped for me." In her poem, death is thoughtful. Much as someone might say, "It's no problem; I'll be glad to stop by your house and pick you up tonight," death does so. He recognizes how busy we are, how much we're trying to fit into so little time. So he says, "That's all right. Don't worry about picking me up on the way to heaven. I'll run by your house. It's on my way." With a sentence, Dickinson defangs death for us. We need to die, she says, even though we might not recognize it or plan for it. How fortunate we are that someone else will take over the details of our dying. Bill did not want to die. I don't want to die. Do you? If it were left to us, we would never find the time. Yet, life is really a matter of death. How we die depends on how we have lived. November is a hard page of the calendar to turn. We've interred the summer under rotting leaves. Will resurrection ever come?

Many deaths overtake us, frustrate us; some we find intolerable or irritating—from losing an umbrella or favorite book or pair of gloves to losing a friend or a home. Then there are those deaths on which God insists—dying to self, dying to bad habits, dying to pride. It's hard to accept all this death. We're not interested in any kind, whether it's the physical death Emily Dickinson had in mind or the spiritual deaths God sends. Yet not a day goes by that we don't face death. An infant relinquishes babyhood to become a toddler, forgets nonsense syllables to learn to speak. Christ talked about a seed dying so that a plant could sprout. Fruit only comes through death. We will only reach our final home, heaven, by dying. Although we know *that*, none of us is anxious to go through death. We don't have time, so we refuse to think about it. Even when our bodies are worn out we resist death.

Fortunately, God doesn't wait for us to get in line for our next good loss. He makes a point of stopping by, as Death does in Dickinson's poem. God knows what we need, and he knows where we belong. When we forget, God remembers.

I t might not be so difficult for us to remember where we belong if we could see our place more clearly. Despite the Bible's ornate descriptions of heaven—roads of gold, choruses, unending joy—it nevertheless holds little meaning for us. How do we prepare for heaven? We might just as easily prepare to become a member of Great Britain's royal family. Yet, heaven is unlike other places we know, for it exists outside of time. It isn't mere extravagance; it is merely God's home. Without God, heaven would cease to be: place and person are inseparable. Occasionally we glimpse what God's place must be like; it happened to me once in Strasbourg, Austria.

The day was gray and glowering, a typical Austrian day in November. I was spending a month in Europe traveling, singing, trying to use my nearly passable German. This Saturday I had traveled by train from Munich to Strasbourg to spend the day. Any part of Austria, friends had told me, was worth seeing.

Overlooking the city was a mountain. A long time ago people had built houses on its side, and I, who am afraid of small hills, wondered how people could live in a place where the floors must slant at a dangerous angle. At the base of the mountain was a beautiful river with paths on either side. There was also a lift of some kind—similar to a ski lift—which took people to the mountain top. The tourist literature bragged about the spectacular view. But no view would make me get into that lift; just writing about it makes my palms sweat.

Instead I opted for a slow, winding walk that ended midway up the mountain. On one side of the path was a sheer drop, with houses below and off in the horizon; on the other side was the rock of mountain. Because the road was only for walkers, and relatively wide, I could stay safely away from the edge. The view of the town was magnificent.

I must have walked for more than half an hour when I rounded another curve similar to all the other curves I had just passed. What greeted me, however, was unlike what I had yet seen. Suddenly the sun broke through the clouds, just as the path widened. To my right was a nunnery, and sweeping the front stoop was a small, wiry nun. Slightly bent over, she looked up as I strode into view, then dismissed me with a wave of her broom: another tourist. To my left, and nearly opposite the nun, were the Swiss Alps—immense, powerful, ageless. At the bend in the road was a stone seat for mesmerized travelers to rest sight and soul. I had to sit. Heaven, I knew, had to be like this, where despite your fears it compells you and holds you in its grip. I understood then why great mountains have always been a symbol for God and his home.

My nun—she had become mine and always would be now—continued her cleaning, barely glancing at me or at the mountains that greeted her every morning. Sweeping her small stoop absorbed all her energy. I found it difficult to imagine a life that contained such a sight every day. Never again would I want this view; as a mortal I was certain I would not know what to do with it if it came. My nun no longer saw the mystery of the Alps. Would heaven become so?

Familiarity and mystery cannot breathe the same air. A glimpse of eternity, a mere shadow of God's face, is all we can accept right now. Once was enough for me, for who can see God's face and live? The longing for it, alone, would drive us mad. Perhaps that's why God did not come to us dressed in Swiss Alps attire but in diapers, a mewling infant. He made it impossible for us to look at him with the unconcerned air of my Austrian nun. Not another mountain, not another god, but one of us, a baby as frail and dependent as any other baby. It's hard to trivialize an infant. The sight of the majestic God will come some day, but not yet, not now. We're not ready.

O f course there may be another way to look at my nun. Perhaps the habit of God had long since ceased to be conscious effort. She did not need to notice the mountains because they had become so much a part of her. There are people who seem to bear the yoke of godliness easily; they have become metaphors for sacrifice, discipline, and commitment. They are my models while I work every day to comfortably wear the habit of God. It takes a lot of relinquishment, a lot of death, to keep the yoke from chafing my shoulders. I'm never ready for November.

So I try to attend and learn well my lessons about mortality, though God isn't tied to any particular classroom. It keeps a student on her toes to recognize when another lesson has begun. It can come anywhere—raking leaves, driving to work, or cooking dinner. Many of my lessons occur in the kitchen since, like my mother, I spend a lot of time there.

Both of us are disasters in the kitchen, not in what we cook but in the way we do it—with cuts and burns and gouges. We're accident-prone. Mother slices herself, not the onions. She burns her hands, not the beans. When my sisters and I came home from school it was common for us to see a big wad of Kleenex or gauze wrapped around Mother's finger, blood oozing through no matter how thick the bandage. "What did you do now?" we'd ask. And she would shrug her shoulders nonchalantly and say, "Oh, I cut my hand," or "Your father sharpened the knives again and didn't tell me." (I can cut myself on a newly sharpened knife right after *I've* been the one to sharpen it; what's my excuse?) It never seemed to matter that she had hurt herself. Although some of those cuts needed stitches, she just wrapped them tight knowing they would heal without a doctor's services: they always did.

There is nothing like seeing a little of our own blood to remind us that dying is our lot. No matter how nutritiously we eat, how much exercise we get, and how well we shrug off stress, we're still going to wear out. In so many different ways we shout, Not So. But once our voices stop, we know the truth. We ought to be grateful that most of us can learn this lesson slowly. We should be glad we don't get everything we want when we want it. If it were the only thing that hadn't gone the way we wanted, it would be even more difficult to die. We're not as fortunate as our agrarian ancestors. For them dying was as common as birth. Farm animals died, crops died, people died: unpleasant but accepted. Now we need symbolic deaths throughout life to teach us the most fundamental human lesson. Those of us who garden see November dying around us. No matter how many Novembers have come and gone, though, it's never easy to watch.

N ovember is also the month of celebration, the month of thanksgiving. It holds a history of triumph er hardship, of gratitude for survival. In November we give thanks: officially, nationally, traditionally. But personally?

Thanksgiving celebrates life in the midst of death. Crops have died to a bounteous display. We've dug potatoes and discarded plants on the compost heap. We've picked the winter squash and set them out to cure. The last of the pole beans, long since shriveled, have sacrificed their seeds for a delicious cassoulet. The lettuce is gone, the tomatoes are canned or juiced. Nothing remains but the feast.

Thanksgiving brightens November and gives us focus. We plan for family and friends to join us, think of new ways to celebrate the day, or cling to each old and lovely tradition. Although fall color is gone, we bring it inside with gourds and dried leaves or the last few mums clinging to their hues, determined not to let frost bleach them brown. We think of the four weeks ahead: Advent, the time of waiting and preparing for the Christchild.

This is one of my favorite times of year (but I say that about every time of year when that time rolls around).

When I think of Thanksgiving I always think of an odor, and with it comes the sight of my mother standing at the stove cooking, stirring, preparing for the day ahead. I can smell it right now. But it wasn't until I cooked my first Thanksgiving dinner that I realized how intensely my memories were tied to my sense of smell, the most primitive and fundamental of our senses. I rose early to prepare the stuffing for the turkey: two kinds, oyster and chestnut, but with the same base. As I began to saute celery in butter, I recognized the odor. All those Thanksgivings were mine again. I stood at the stove in my mother's place, all because of a little butter and celery.

As we grow older we find ourselves unconsciously, sometimes consciously, standing where our parents stood and behaving as they did. We may even come to want to do so. By standing in their place we connect ourselves to them—and to our grandparents and great-grandparents. We are more than a single life; we are part of life that continues even after death. Losing a parent is hard for just that reason. When Allen's father died in November, suddenly Allen was the last generation, the older generation to his children. His link beyond himself disappeared. I don't want to consider my parents' death any more than Allen wanted to consider his father's, but to learn how to become the older generation, I must. We can't start to learn this too early. I began that day as I cooked celery in butter.

Because my family related thanksgiving not only to a secular feast but to a worship service, the scent of sauteing celery also reminds me of my connection to God. I am his creature, as well as my parents.' I stand in God's tradition of sacrifice and celebration, of death and Passover and remembrance, as well as that of my country's founders. I am a Christian, as well as an American.

Each of us has scents that trigger memory, emotion, and worship, whether it be smelling candles or inhaling incense. For others the scent of paste wax or grape juice might hint of holidays, family traditions, or attitudes unconsidered for years. Our lives are filled with odors that our mental noses store away, forever associated with a particular activity. God can use those memories to help us focus our minds and hearts on him, to return us to calmer days when worship was a matter of being, not a catch-as-catch-can affair. My mother cleared space for worship and made it central; worship *was* the feast, was life. Now I need to clear the space myself, often a difficult task with numerous demands drawing me from the clearing.

I was young when the smells of Thanksgiving were fresh. Now, they poignantly remind me not only of family and worship but of mortality. Then, I was unaware of the constancy of death; I never considered my own death or that of my parents. Each day would always resemble the previous day, each Thanksgiving reflect all the other Thanksgivings I had known. Yet some traditions have died so that others might live.

It is difficult to give up any traditions, even in little things. Although each year I try to vary the Thanksgiving menu, my husband won't have it: Everything must remain the same. The sameness started with my parents and continues with my sisters and brother—the same stuffing recipes, the same vegetables and pies, the same pickles and olives. Although Allen doesn't come from a particularly tradition-conscious family, he adamantly adheres to our traditions.

Each generation, though, must make its own. We may follow the same menu my parents have used for years on Thanksgiving, but the remainder of Thanksgiving resembles nothing I knew as a child. We have a recorder concert, the one time of the year when Allen and our friends play the instrument; I usually serve as audience. We drag out the music, set up the music stands, and tune up—as much as a person can tune a recorder. Kathy, my sister-in-law, who has perfect pitch, finds it agonizing to play a recorder that refuses to stay in tune. But Thanksgiving brings out the persistence in people. Although I don't play, I look forward to the hilarity of listening to others try. I enjoy it almost as much as those who play the music, and it has come to mark the beginning of the Advent-Christmas season as much as cooking celery or eating oyster stuffing and pumpkin pie.

Traditions are made of things our senses can understand—tastes, sounds, and smells. I no longer awaken to the scent of celery since we don't spend the holiday with my family. So if there are to be any odiforous memories and traditions made in my house, I am the one to make them for others, in the same spirit, I hope, that my mother made them for me. Whether or not they translate into a sense of worship and gratitude is not up to me. But it helps if mouth and hands, as well as nose, eyes, and ears, are filled with the sounds, sights, tastes, smells, and touches of love. I give this to you out of love, we say—this bread, this wine, this song, this cup, this body, broken for you.

Sometimes gifts of love must be broken. Sometimes death and life intermingle, as they do in November—a month that starts with death and ends anticipating life. When the pilgrims first celebrated Thanksgiving, they were acknowledging both death and life, grieving for their friends who had died and praising God that some of them had survived. In the church year, Thanksgiving leans toward Advent, anticipating the Incarnation. November contains the whole cycle of human existence.

My father-in-law died in November, but in November my father was born.

3   December Waiting

N o month hovers quite so much as December. Children, certainly, wait none-too-patiently for the end of the month. But adults also experience the weight of waiting. In my part of the country, days have settled into their winter rhythm, wrapped in their winter garb. Sunday gray is daily best; and it always looks like snow. But waiting does not necessarily mean inactivity. Part of waiting is preparation.

Holiday preparations drain people when they don't wait actively. Because December is not a rushing kind of month, I try to fit my rhythm and mood with the weather. This month becomes almost stodgy in its insistence on one way—an occasional hint of the sun, just to remind us that light has not entirely left the world. The heavy clouds in the chill air and the low, low sky keep me steadily on course. December doesn't deliver daydreaming weather or hibernating weather; it brooks no postponing.

My Scandinavian family waited actively, particularly

when it came to Christmas baking. I now begin almost immediately after Thanksgiving. Each weekend I bake a few batches of cookies, freezing them in Christmas tins until the holidays arrive. Although I'm not fond of baking cookies, at Christmas the refrigerating, rolling, and shaping of the dough seems a fitting tradition, a special way of waiting for the celebration to begin. I give cookies to neighbors; I offer them to guests; I try to keep my family from eating too many at once.

A celebration should not come easily or it's not a celebration; it fails to have meaning. True, we can celebrate with grilled cheese and a glass of water, but a full-fledged party demands something special—petits fours, fruit-cake, foie gras. We need to work and prepare, to sacrifice time and energy before the celebration arrives. When we try to cram that into a few days or even a few hours, how can we wonder when we become frustrated or irritated, maybe even a little angry at a season that demands too much of us. That way the celebration becomes an imposition, rather than the joy for which we have longed.

When we wait and prepare, we can come to the feast rested, enthusiastic. But there is an even greater, benefit: In daily preparation we keep the purpose of the feast constantly before us. We remember why we shop for that special gold, frankincense, or myrrh to give our loved ones. Each newly frozen batch of cookies says, "This is for the feast; this is for the mother and child." The funeral food has turned into party favorites, the best birthday party we've ever attended.

Our work is also a reflection of God's work. He didn't stint on the preparations, and he spent a lot longer on them than we ever do. First came the prophets, then came John, and finally Mary's nine long months and lowly labor surrounded by God's loving creatures. So we dust the corner where the tree will stand and carefully unwrap each ornament. It's our way of getting ready.

I have a problem with cookies, though, at least the kind I bake—all that butter. The arteries of too many Americans are also known for too much butter—and meat and fried foods. Most of us eat far too much fat. December is a particularly hard month to keep our triglyceride and cholesterol levels down. Besides butter-laden cookies, there's eggnog and standing rib roast and shrimp and plum pudding, goose and duck. It's a fat-enriched tradition.

Our spiritual diets aren't much better. We gobble easy Christianity bloated with mutual funds and stock portfolios, beautiful clothes and me-first fashions. Nor are we much good at spiritual exercises. We would rather gorge ourselves on superfluous spiritual fads and feel-good formulas than strengthen ourselves on the complex carbohydrates of the gospel: Feed the hungry. Clothe the cold. Support your enemies. Sacrifice your time and money. Expend your energy exercising for others. Prepare the way of the Lord.

Prepare is the verb of Advent. Fat is the enemy of preparation. We don't have the strength to carve out the way for God's coming because we carry too much fat around with us. Look at John the Baptist's diet: nuts, berries, locusts, and the Old Testament prophet Isaiah. Not too much fat there. Maybe he was on to something.

Here lies the tension of Advent, the four weeks before Christmas. Advent is set in the center of secular life. We make Advent wreaths and light Advent candles, read the prophets and remember God's promises.

The one who will ransom captive Israel, Emmanuel, is coming. If only he'd hurry. Our celebration occurs in a heavy time of year. The coming of spring would heighten the anticipation for the Incarnation. But the Church determined to remember the Nativity during a season of hibernation: short days, long nights, sleepy people—a time to catch us nodding as we watch. So we try to keep sleep away by activities that focus our thoughts on what is to come.

But cookies and candles can't always do it. If the verb of Advent is *prepare*, the adverb is *repentantly*. Advent was never intended to be a raucous time of year. Cookies and wassail cheer us artificially. The Prophets and the best of our carols ask, "why do we need this baby?" What have we done to deserve him? He is judge as well as redeemer. In fact, he cannot redeem until he does judge. What will he find? We've eaten too many cookies; we've failed to understand November's lesson of dying; we've waited impatiently or not at all. Advent is our last chance of the year to understand the significance of the quiet feast, the somber celebration. It is no light word the Prophets give us. God is coming. Get ready to greet him. Break out the frozen cookies.

No, the cookies aren't for him; they're for the people we'll invite to the birthday party. We won't need anything special for his entourage either, because he won't have one. Just his mother and stepfather will be coming. What will God want to eat? Nothing more than what his mother can supply. It all sounds pretty bizarre; but that's what we're waiting for: God, the helpless infant, the ruler, the judge, the redeemer. Turn up the heat; it's cold outside, and God's only wearing swaddling clothes. Besides, it's beginning to snow. . . .

I 've lived in northern climates most of my life and loved every snowfall I've seen. I always celebrate the first few inches that accumulate. Why would someone want to stay inside just because of a little snow?

My sisters and brother and I never did. No matter how long it took to get into snowsuits, boots, scarfs, hats, and mittens, we wanted to be outside making snowmen or snow angels. We wanted to be iceskating or sledding. Every so often Mother would come to the door and yell, "Aren't you cold? Shouldn't you come in now?"

Eventually we had to come in either to eat or because our snowsuits really were too wet to wear any longer. Mother always greeted us with one question: "Are you in now?" meaning "Have you had enough? Are you inside to stay?" We always assured her we were. So she took our clothes and spread them to dry on every available radiator throughout the house. Mother knew us. She knew it wouldn't be long before we asked, "Are our clothes dry?" (We didn't count a little dampness.) Cabin fever was not a childhood disease; kids who stayed indoors were sissies.

Mother never treated winter as an enemy to be conquered. She never lost her childlike enthusiasm for the first snowfall—or the last. We wanted snow—an essential forerunner of Christmas, a part of waiting. There is no silence like a late night snowfall in December, a silence filled with promise.

December is a barren time of year; it begins the time for resting, when trees and plants lie dormant. December is as necessary as sleep at night. But without snow the earth would be brown and barren. It drapes conifers and evergreens; it buries bulbs and hosta beneath its insulating care. Without a good spring snow melt, plants fail to get the start they need.

Mother always told us that when we complain about

the weather, we complain about God. When I grumble about rain or cold, I remember her words. Yet, life contains days as bitter and turbulent as a snowstorm. To complain of them is to complain of the weather of the soul. Jesus faced the cold dressed in swaddling clothes. We at least have the luxury of thermolactyl underwear, snowsuits, and boots from L. L. Bean. We can cover cold hands with polypropylene. It's possible, now, to be warmer than ever before. But we seem so much colder. We resist God's weather; we fight the blizzards, anguish over the ice. Dressed as we are we should be able to rest easily. Yet if there is an image in all our faith that says, "Don't fret," it is the infant lying in a manger. Whether we live in warm climates or cold, each of us experiences the chill of December—each of us waits when it is all we can do. And this is a blessing.

All of us can learn to relish the beauty of waiting silently. Every December God insists that we wait, storing up the nutrients we need. Don't fight December, he says. Rather, mold yourself to it. Conform yourself to my shape, hear my melody, learn my rhythm.

Just as snow is essential, so is music in this season. Although I find it hard to choose a favorite piece, some in their structure and text reflect waiting much more clearly than do others; they settle silence on the soul. If I had to choose, it would be "Of the Father's Love Begotten," which in just a few verses sums up the whole of God's overwhelming love for us. It is thoroughly theological, unerringly orthodox. The simple words are austere in their beauty; they *must* be to match the melody of plainsong.

Plainsong is a seamless, sweeping swell. It curves, it turns, it rises, it falls—all without stopping. Plainsong is the living sound of God's love, endless, effortless, unadorned because itself is the adornment. Plainsong is music to live in, the easiest sound to wear. In plainsong the glory of God's heavenly love rings with dignity and inevitability. It sounds the way snow looks.

Branches shrouded in snow lose their angularity, their shrill appearance. Snow hushes the insistent crack and rasp of bare limbs rubbing against one another in the winter wind. The landscape of snow becomes a plainsong, a soft chant to us and to God. Snow and song beckon us to modulate our tones to those of the earth around us. "Soft, this is a sleeping land, a waiting land, a whispering land"; we are to sleep and rest and whisper our plainsong too.

Advent is a searchlight into our souls, a time to surrender our souls to silence. What do we find there? We will find sin, but sin can be whiter than snow. The Bible doesn't accidentally use the image of snow to explain what happens to sin when God walks in. Perhaps that is why plainsong seems to me so particularly appropriate during Advent. It pierces the soul's center, bringing serenity. Although we may be baking cookies, wrapping presents, or struggling with what to give a special person, plainsong brings us back to the fundamentals. "Of the Father's love begotten Ere the worlds began to be, He is Alpha and Omega, He the source, the ending he, Of the things that are, that have been, And that future years shall see, Evermore and evermore."

D ecember is so contradictory. Often the silence in our hearts and minds drowns out the clattering pots and pans or the scraping shovel on the sidewalk. We wait for the twenty-one-inch, eight-and-a-half-pound baby boy, probably the only time all year when Jesus is so much a part of everything we do. Some also wait for snow or presents. Others wait to begin preparations. Still others wait impatiently to surprise their family. That is the hardest kind of waiting for me.

December is the month I need most of all the twelve, because I'm so bad at waiting for surprises. I dread this month and love it at the same time. When I was growing up, I always wanted to know exactly what people were giving me for Christmas. Mother loved to surprise us. I made life particularly hard for her in December. No matter where she hid the presents, I almost always found them. I instigated search parties, insisting that Stephanie be a scout too. Although she would have been content to wait, a big sister is a big sister. Yet, I remember Christmases when mother did surprise me; I will never forget the joy on her face.

I have seldom tried to surprise anyone, though I succeeded once with Allen. He fell in love with a piece of needlepoint I made for my brother Steven on his birthday a few years ago. It was St. George slaying the dragon, the design based on an ancient Russian icon. For months after Steven took George to Chicago, Allen moaned about it. "You'll never make another one, will you?" he asked me over and over. He knows I dislike repeating myself; and he knows George took several months to complete. But I decided that for Christmas I would make him a George. I stitched the piece at the office. Working on breaks and lunches, I took four months to finish it. For two weeks prior to Christmas I arrived at the office extra early and stayed late. Once I finished stitching, it still had to be blocked and framed. I finished it with two days to spare. Although my friends kept telling me to wrap it unfinished, I couldn't. With every stitch I thought how Allen would respond when he unwrapped it. It was everything I'd hoped for.

Allen's confused look, his questions—"Where did this come from? Why did Steven give George back? You mean, it's for me?"—held nearly every emotion the shepherds felt the night of Jesus' birth. The shock and surprise of the shepherds must have made it all worthwhile for God. Their visit confirmed to Mary the wonder

of what God had done with her. We're still surprised.
Our faces reflect amazement that a baby can be our sal-
vation. Babies need care, security, warmth; they aren't
the ones to care for others or make others secure. We
would never look for the presents of grace and sacrifice
in a crib. If God wanted to surprise us, he couldn't have
picked a better hiding place than a baby in diapers lying
in a hay trough next to some cows and a few smelly
sheep. Not even I would have thought to look there.

God shows such marvelous imagination in the way
Jesus came to us. We've felt the charm and poignancy
of it for thousands of years; even those who have no
belief cannot remain unaffected by it. From the creation
to Christmas, God displayed his speciality—the unexpected, the unusual. He displayed his ingenuity and
inventiveness. He anticipates Christmas in ways we
would never imagine, giving us hints, teasing us with
just-you-waits and pretty-soon-nows.

Then comes Christmas Eve, the climax of our waiting.
We have a last chance to repent, to cleanse ourselves of
all unrighteousness: Christmas Eve, the final preparation
before the coming of our Lord. No other time is like it,
not Maundy Thursday, not Good Friday, not Easter.
Everything stems from Christmas Eve, the night of Incarnation—God's great, radical, unexpected plan. Imagine
God as our friend, sharing with us a burger and a shake.
Or better, a tofu salad, bran muffin, and glass of skim
milk. "I'd like you to meet someone," we say to an ac-
quaintance. "This is Jesus, lately of heaven, now living
down the street." No, it's too difficult a scene.

But on Christmas Eve the impossible, the unimagin-
able happens. We light the candles, tune our hearts to
the coming great event, and remember. As we honor
that messy manger scene, we sanctify it. We hover—all
of us in churches everywhere—on the edge of the greatest event in history, the beginning of our faith. It silences
us. Now, even the slowest of us say "So that's the

surprise." A baby. God's son. And then we remember the rest of the story, the part the shepherds didn't know, as we partake of communion.

The beginning and the ending are united in this one act: God's incarnation and his sacrifice, his sinlessness and our sinfulness. In reenacting the Eucharist now, we enter the festivities through the narrow gate, the only gate. We pledge that we are in love and charity with our neighbors; we commit our lives to holy, righteous, and sober living for the service of our Lord and his kingdom. Those are awesome vows, and necessary. We cannot welcome the Lord to our earth and our homes and our hearts if we do not do so for everyone, sinners all. Now we find the gift worth waiting for, just as the shepherds did.

Yet we aren't shepherds—frightened, cold, tired—on the move to Bethlehem. We can't touch the infant Jesus or listen to his quiet breathing. Christmas Eve yields to Christmas Day, only a commemoration, not the original. Although we long to pick up the child and give him his first teddy bear and congratulate Mary and Joseph, we can't. So we we pour another steaming mug of coffee and think of the holy family, of our holy families, near and far.

We see it all, staring into the fire, but Jesus and his family don't share our flames. Remembering isn't enough. Our hands and feet long for physical activity, for giving and receiving, for exchanging and delighting in the exchange. We need the mystery the shepherds experienced. Christmas calls for early-morning whispers and sleepy-eyed wonder.

I want to be up and whispering as the shepherds were long ago. Now is no time for rest. The waiting has ended.

4   January Just in Time

D ecember should end with Christmas. No one
thinks of New Year's Eve when he thinks of
December. New Year's Eve is part of January; Christmas,
part of December. But that's the way the official calendar
reads.

Each of us, though, has an internal calendar. It may
not agree with the one from Audubon—the calendar
your great-aunt gave you for Christmas, not knowing
that birds were your least favorite animal and you really
would have preferred one with cats. You may be ready
for spring training this month, though you know it
doesn't start for another six weeks. Maybe you're ready
to sort through last year's spring and summer wardrobe.
For you, Easter is right around the corner.

What does a person *do* in January? Plenty, when we
spend it contemplating what January is all about—time.
No month so preoccupies itself with itself as January
does. It starts calling attention to time from New Year's
Eve onward.

There's no particular reason for time to start at midnight on January 1, any more than there's a reason why each new day should start at 12:01 A.M. But somebody somewhere decided we needed some order, so we have sixty seconds to a minute, sixty minutes to an hour, twenty-four hours to a day, approximately thirty days to a month, twelve months to a year, ten years to a decade, and so on. It's a lot better than it was when each town or group of people set their own time. Travel would have been tough. (Did you know that it wasn't until this century that France finally came in line with the rest of us on Greenwich mean time? Naturally the French thought mean time should originate in France). Daniel Boorstin in *The Discoverers* declares that ordering time was the first great discovery of Western civilization. When we add up all the hours in a month or even in a week (yes, the sum is more than forty) we have an astounding figure, lots of hours to waste or redeem. Where do they go? How much time can we have on our hands?

In part of our house, we've solved the time problem by banishing it. The clock on our family room wall reads two minutes after five, because that's when I unplugged it years ago. The clock would work if I plugged it in, but I won't, because people would complain. My yellow wall clock must be the noisiest clock around. It hums and buzzes and snorts and burps, constantly calling attention to itself, rather like New Year's Eve announcing January over and over again. There is not a more irritating way to hear time pass than to listen to that clock. I always ignored it; our family room makes it easy to ignore time anyway. For me, Gustav Mahler or Merle Haggard ably drowned out that clock's hiccups. But people kept asking me, "How can you stand that clock?" Being a quick translator, I knew they were really saying, "I can't stand that clock." So one day I unplugged it. Yet I left it on the wall, probably because the wall would look strange without something there and I had no better substitute. So it hangs, two minutes after five, no matter what the hour of day or night, no matter what the season of the year, no matter how quickly time outside approaches midnight on New Year's Eve.

For the most part, a stopped clock doesn't present any problems—until I forget that the clock isn't running and glance its way to check the time. I'm always startled that the time never varies. Two minutes after five. Although I caused it, I'm startled nonetheless. Then I'm irritated that I have such a stupid clock doing me absolutely no good. A clock isn't a painting; it's functional—or it should be. Yet I either have a clock that unremittingly gurgles "Time is passing," or I have one that has passed into eternity.

Most of the time I prefer it plugged into eternity. Time moves swiftly enough without having that fact reinforced every second. I am not a cuckoo clock type of person. God's way of tolling time is enough for me—the four seasons, night and day. I can also accept the Church's way: Advent and Epiphany, Lent, Easter, Ascension, Pentecost, the beginning at the end, calendars ready to turn (or in my case already turned) to January. For the Church, the world is just beginning, life is just about to be born, how silently, how silently. The heavy air and gray skies muffle the sound of that first infant cry, the first shushing sound the mother makes. That's the most beautiful way to mark time.

My yellow clock hangs in the appropriate room, because our family room has no windows. It was once an ordinary, unfinished basement, I suppose, which a previous owner paneled and carpeted. But the fireplace is large and warming; burning thorn apple makes the air tasty. When we first thought of buying this house, the family room oppressed us—no windows, dark carpeting, even darker paneling. Now we find the room soothing. Although the room is dark, it isn't like night. To enter our family room is to enter eternity.

In its immediacy we make time any time we choose. It might be January outside, but inside? That's the beauty of our room, as well as the beauty of January: We can skate or ski one minute and the next enter another time or place or era. We can, and do, plan our spring garden in front of the fireplace, though it must be a particularly anti-garden day, a day twenty-eight degrees below zero, when neither car will start and we're forced indoors and downstairs. We don't know whether our perennials will survive that kind of cold. Western lower Michigan is in zone five or six (depending on the catalog or map you study, good for perennials until ten below). When we dip as low as twenty-eight below, we are thankful for snow cover, nature's insulation which ensures that in the spring and summer we will have flowers to tend. But rather than worry that every peony would need to be replaced, we envision our vegetable garden, flourishing, ripening, feeding us (and some of our neighbors) with carrots and squash, tomatoes and corn, peas and lettuce and spinach. As we order our seeds we see new shoots pushing out of moist, warm earth. We anticipate the first fishing trip of the season and know we'd better prepare for vacation. All of these—gardens and fish and vacations—are aspects of God's grace. Our winter room, too, reflects God's provision, a place to go when there's no place to go.

We can go anywhere in our imaginations. We can be in a concert hall listening to Bach's unaccompanied partitas—achingly beautiful music—or at the opera house applauding the opening strains of *Der Rosenkavalier*. Or if the down-home mood prevails, we fly to Austin, Texas, for a little Willie Nelson. Where else can we go? We can also go to God.

Jesus told his disciples to enter a closet or small room to pray. In other words, each of us needs a place to go when there's nowhere else, some place where time holds no meaning. In such a place there are no distractions to prevent us moving with God to where he wants us to be. The heart of forgiveness? The hallway of healing? The room of mercy? These are the places we visit when time no longer presses and January takes from us the ability or desire to move. For me, having been healed in front of the fireplace, I am able to forgive and be forgiven more easily than before I sat down.

We don't think enough about the necessity of forgiveness, perhaps because we don't spend enough time outside of time. If we're unused to January, it might take more than a still afternoon for God to suck from our marrow the incessant beat that minutes, seconds, and milliseconds make. It might take a day or two, a week, or even the entire month. We so easily remember the slights and hurts people have given us; but how difficult to think of those hurts when we sit at God's place rather than ours.

That's what takes the timelessness. There is much to be said for having a great deal to forgive. It gives us a perspective from eternity, a glimpse of God's job description. Although we may not want the view, we need it. He who has more to forgive than any of us glories in it. God gleefully and joyously forgives us—over and over again—each time we come to him truthfully and honestly confessing our stupidity, our sins, our petty-mindedness, our pride. He forgives pride the most up-roariously of all because it's the one hardest for us to hand over. It's Bilbo's ring—"Here, take it. No? Didn't I give it to you? It couldn't still be in my pocket," we say with the hobbit. Pride has a way of slipping back into our pocket every time we try to take it out. Can we forgive others as God forgives us, as though there is no greater pleasure in this world than forgiving? It might take more than January to learn how. It might take a lifetime of no place to go, nothing to do, and no time to do it in. But once we've learned how, we can enter time again, confident that we can practice that timeless discipline of forgiveness.

T he hours of January can oppress someone who is uncomfortable with no place to go or who doesn't enjoy enforced solitude. January, as with December, as with most of our months—most of our lives—is a time of contradictions. What to one person is just the right time to stay indoors is to another the best time to be outside. Some people complain that winter has gone on long enough; others want a few more months of skiing. As Garrison Keillor so fondly points out, people in northern climates brag about how much cold weather they can endure. Bearing the cold is a badge of manhood, a mark of endurance beyond the average human being, an acceptance of the amusing—cold—ways of God. "Oh yes, it's a cold one," we mutter. We use the same tone of voice on the deepest summer day when we say, "It's a hot one." Living in the extremes of life, whether it's temperature or adversity, creates character. Western Michigan certainly can't boast the extremes of Lake Wobegon, Minnesota—we're not far enough north—but we've had our share. This year, for the first time in several, we're "having winter." Everywhere I go, in grocery stores and gas stations, I hear people say, "Yup, we've got winter now."

We're skittish when it comes to winter. In recent years the calendar has belied the weather. What we thought would be winter, what we'd hoped would be winter, what we bought our snowthrowers, snowmobiles, cross country skis, and ice skates for, never happened. The weather toyed with us, teasing us into hopes that have remained unfulfilled. A day of slightly below freezing—hopes high—then warm, slushy weather in the forties and rain, rain, rain—hopes low. Winter has behaved too much like coy spring to put much stock in it. But finally our long-awaited winter is here.

God has been dishing out his marvelous season, well-spiced, for days now: two-plus feet of snow, cold cob-web-clearing air, slick ice, and all the excuses a person would ever need to warm his frosty toes and hands by a fire, wrap an afghan over his winter woolens, and read. Faced with record cold temperatures, some people, I'm sure, choose to watch football rather than words on a page. Although I do some of each, a book is the better bargain. I'm not against outdoor activity in winter; I love to jog, walk, ski, or skate no matter how cold. News reports warning of frostbite and urging us to stay indoors make January sound perilous to our health. Although it isn't, provided we dress correctly, we probably won't want to spend more than four—or eight—hours out-doors in below zero temperature and winds above twenty or thirty miles an hour without eventually return-ing home. But while we're out sweeping clear our minds, we also have the marvelous prospect of hot chocolate and a fire. It's as great a pleasure as swimming in a cold lake on a hot, hot day in summer.

With all the marvels we've invented to keep ourselves warm when it's cold, we don't need to stay indoors in winter. Nor will we necessarily be cold once we leave the fireside; it doesn't take long to warm up while shovel-ing snow, skating, skiing, or chopping wood. In fact, the body uses oxygen more efficiently during cold weather activity than in warm weather exertion. That's a good enough reason to leave the chore of chopping wood until it's cold, and to use the remaining warm fall weather for fishing and harvesting. But as far as winter temperatures are concerned, how it affects us depends on how we prepare, as well as the attitude with which we approach it: It doesn't take long to love skiing or skating.

O ur frozen creek makes for good skating, almost as good as the pond in Connecticut where I learned to skate. The character of Connecticut Yankees must be forged by ice skating. My mother couldn't keep me or Stephanie away from the pond. We trudged down the street, around the corner, across a friend's lawn, and then through the woods, our skates clanging across our shoulders all the while. When we saw the clearing ahead, we knew we were near. Sitting on any available, semi-dry log, we put on our skates. We'd even sit right in the snow if all logs were occupied. What was a slightly damp seat? We were bound to get even wetter before we finished skating. We had no warming house, candy machines, or lockers for our stuff, as we did where I skated every day at lunch when I lived and worked outside of Chicago. We didn't need anything fancy except a couple of pairs of socks and our skates. Nor did we worry about our things; who would steal somebody else's shoes? (Maybe hide them for a joke—but steal them?) When we got too hungry or cold, Stephanie and I returned home; but that stage took a long time to reach. Once we were on the ice we never wanted to leave. She and I skated for hours—nothing fancy, no spins or jumps or twists, just plain, old-fashioned skating in the clean Connecticut air.

I remember that pond as huge. Probably it wasn't, though it seemed large enough for long lines of big kids to play whip (I was about eight at the time). My only ambition then was to grow up to be twelve or fourteen so I could get in line, perhaps to be thrown on the ice or into a snow bank. By the time I was the right age, I no longer lived in Connecticut but in Pennsylvania, another cold winter climate. There I skated on the Yellow Breeches River, which wandered for miles in and out of the woods and was always crowded with kids, especially on weekends; the worst weekends were those right before exams. Who wanted to study on a sunny, cold Sunday with the ice just right and the blades sharp? I certainly didn't, as I'm sure my science or math exams showed. "Let's go skating this afternoon" were words heard all over church, never, "Let's go to the movies." Who wanted to stay indoors?

I want to spend the hours of January in two ways—stay indoors and dream, or go outdoors and dream. Only in January can different activities have the same result. Skating is like floating or flying but with feet comfortably attached to the earth. The sensation remains in our muscles and marrow long after we stop. People walk differently, having skated, head and shoulders more erect.

Skating always reminds me of prayer. When we have talked deeply with God and breathed his air, his oxygen takes awhile to leave our cells. Eventually, we return to normal, just as the motion of skating eventually wears off. We have the memory, though, of what prayer was like, how our cells and spirits sang with unearthly oxygen. That should be enough to send us back to God, but, being perverse people, it isn't always. We need something to jar us, something as cobweb-clearing as skating. Every rasp of blade on ice intones a prayer for me. A world that contains ice and trees and skates deserves some attention; the creator who made them deserves some thanks.

And so I encourage people to skate in the winter— adults who have forgotten the ordinary, everyday, energy-building pleasures. Skating is a matter of rhythm and relaxation, not being afraid to fall, being willing to glide rather than walk. That first skate of the year is glorious, even if as I skate I must shovel snow to clear the ice. And each outing is as glorious as the one before, whether I skate alone or with others. Midday skating, even if only for half an hour, is especially welcome to those who work deskbound. It is time better spent than with a cheeseburger, fries, and á shake. Skating is a help to health—physical, mental, and spiritual. The extra oxygen we breathe seems to purify problems and dissolve worry and tension. There are lots of activities, of course, that provide the same benefits, but not many as fun.

I 'm not usually anxious for one month to end and another to begin. Seasons are short enough without always longing for another. Sometimes I wish nature had been ordered so that we enjoyed four six-month periods, not that nature is as neatly divided into quarters as are businesses. One year fall may last into December, while in another it may end in October. That keeps us from boredom.

I try to resist all attempts at universal summer. California and Florida truck farmers are particularly guilty of this, shipping us summer produce now at a price too dear for most of us to afford. As much as I love these foods, I don't want strawberries and peaches in January anyway, or asparagus before spring. Just as I want to live seasonally, not escaping January for Florida and July, I want to eat seasonally as well. I feel the same about flowers. Although I love anticipating my field of daffodils, don't bring me one in January.

A secretary once bought a bunch of yellow daffodils and gave a flower to each of us—in anticipation and longing for spring, she said. Without thinking I replied, "But I'm not ready for spring. I'm still having winter." I was ungracious. Yet, that bright yellow face was too seductive; I knew I could easily be swayed from my path to view even a single flower with equanimity.

Maybe I was secretly ready for spring, no matter how much I loved winter. Maybe I was ready for infidelity. Maybe that flower proved too great a temptation. For hadn't I given the new garden catalogs, so bright and fertile, to my husband to file away until the February doldrums struck? (February is the hardest month of the year for me; I'm always grateful it's the shortest.) Hadn't I wanted to take just a few peeks at the new vegetable offerings from Burpee, compare prices on potato eyes, and revel in the best prose and brightest flowers that catalogs have to offer in the new edition from White Flower Farm? Hadn't I longed to spend my credit certificate from Wayside Gardens as soon as I saw that glorious clematis on the cover? And hadn't my husband absolutely said, "No, you can't look at these yet"?

Even with the best intentions, we find it difficult to be faithful to the present. We always want to be somewhere else at some other time. If only I were younger but knew what I know; every adult has said that a time or two; every teenager determines that he never will. Wanting to be where we aren't is an inescapable part of nature. We might call it a fatal flaw. Certainly it was fatal for Eve and Adam; it's been congenital ever since. We're such restless, ungrateful, faithless creatures. *Now* never looks so good as what's to come or as marvelous as our yesterdays.

Lots of times we think that if only we'd been here yesterday or if only we would come back tomorrow, we'd have more excitement. Every fisherman knows what I'm talking about: "Yesterday they were really biting." We live believing the White Queen's rule: Jam tomorrow and jam yesterday, but never jam today. What makes her rule so apt, and so amusing, is that it's so true. Each of us knowingly nods his head. (Actually it comes in handy with kids who do want to eat jam more than is good for them; all I need to say is "Remember the White Queen's rule" and I hear it recited, all requests ceasing. Try it sometime.) But in one area, the jam rule doesn't work—the area of God's grace. He's a yesterday, tomorrow, and a today God. His grace operates at all times, most particularly now. We can remember his actions; we can anticipate the future; but we only know his grace in the present, so to wish for anything other than now is to deny ourselves grace. We have no other place to live than now, the only place where God's grace lives. If only we were there, too, we would know it.

Of course, *now* shifts around so that it's hard to become accustomed to it. Just when we think we've got now in hand, now changes, which is part of the challenge—and fun—of living. We've figured out the hours of January—the hours for meditation, the hours for activity, the cold hours, the hours in front of the fireplace. And then January shrugs and throws off its winter hours with a thaw. January reaches high, a day or three of forty-plus degree weather. Meltdown begins. But January thaws don't always happen in January—another frustrating thing about the present. Sometimes they come in February; sometimes they never arrive. But last weekend when Allen and I were jogging, there was an unusual scent in the air, a scent, almost, of spring.

Nature tricks us at this time of year, and the gardening catalog people participate with nature in the deception. Such warm weather, coupled with the arrival of Burpee, Gurney, and the rest, make us think that tomorrow spring will be here—not three months from tomorrow. I almost see my crocus and daffodil bulbs sprouting from the ground, even though we still have more than a foot of snow. I have to shake my head to see, instead, the slush and remaining patches of ice the sun has not yet found.

The memory of my field of daffodils is so strong. Will it be as beautiful as last year? Then I think "no jam today"; somehow things never seem as lovely as we remember them. What about the dozens of crocus bulbs I planted last fall? Will they come up? Did I plant them too shallow? (I did, I know it.) Bulbs are the most mysterious and frustrating of plants. You bury them in the fall and wait months before you know what's happened. Other plants let a gardener know quickly if they like their home, though even plants that appear dead can spring to life provided the root system is healthy. Not only are bulbs buried deep in the ground, a half foot or more, but they need cold weather; the colder the winter, the more beautiful the spring show.

A January thaw is a tease. The longer it lasts the more we're drawn into the deception. It plays on our desire to want something other than now; before we know it we're living in the future, not the present. Yet in a day or two, January clutches its hours back around itself, often with hauteur, as if to say what doltish, gullible creatures we are. With a wry sigh, we admit how right January is.

5 February Sacrifice

W hen I was growing up in Connecticut, a person was either Catholic or Baptist. There wasn't much in between.

Those were the days, the late fifties, when Catholics still took their faith seriously, at least the outward forms: fish on Friday, confession on Saturday, mass on Sunday, periodic fast days, feast days, parades, and Lent. Baptists prided themselves that they had no outward evidences of faith. Our faith showed in what we didn't do—drinking, dancing, smoking, playing cards. It's tough to recognize a person's faith by the fact that he isn't playing cards. But that's the way we wanted it. Catholics, though, were intriguing, mysterious, compelling people with lots of things to watch; I wanted to get a close look without falling into empty ritual.

I was in seventh grade, finally released from childhood and one room, one teacher. School no longer gave us much time for boredom; fifty minutes and we were off somewhere else. As I recall, the first class of the day was penmanship (yes, we still had penmanship—the Palmer method). Our room was organized into three groups of desks, rather like pews in a church, two desks to a group, in long rows front to back. I sat in the right-hand desk of the middle group about three rows from the front. Across the narrow aisle sat an orange-headed, freckle-faced Irish boy, the quintessential Irish Catholic. Although I can't remember his name—I think it was Michael—I remember clearly what he looked like, especially that Ash Wednesday. His mother let him come to school with a dirty face—a big, black smudge right in the middle of his forehead.

As a Baptist, I didn't celebrate any special kind of day (except church twice on Sunday, Wednesday evening prayer meeting, Thursday junior choir rehearsal, and Friday youth fellowship). I had forgotten, if I had ever known, that Ash Wednesday began the most solemn part of the church year: Lent. On Ash Wednesday observant Catholics attended mass for the imposition of ashes, and then they fasted. Michael probably had little more understanding of the imagery than I did. He was obviously embarrassed that he had to spend the day with a sooty forehead. Nor was he excited about the fasting part. Probably he wasn't looking forward to giving up something for Lent. I know I wouldn't have been.

But that was in seventh grade. Now I understand a little better why the ashes, why the fasting, why the self-imposed sacrifice for the forty days before the Resurrection. Although I don't attend church on Ash Wednesday, I am conscious when Lent begins, that season representing Jesus' forty-day temptation in the desert. For several years now I have given up something, as my Catholic friends used to say back in junior high. It's nothing compared to what Christ gave up when he walked the road to Golgotha, but at least I'm on the right path.

I don't know what I'll find in the desert of Lent this year, this desert that is my soul, this desert that is my need for spiritual food and drink. I know that the desert is dusty dry; my tongue thickens at the thought. I know that my feet will throb from the pain of prickly pear, which pierces my shoes and bloodies my flesh. I know that stones make very poor bread; how I will long for a fresh brown loaf just out of the oven.

I know what Jesus found—hunger and thirst and temptation. He found Satan lurking for him, teasing him, tantalizing him, promising him power, the one thing Jesus had forsaken when he left heaven for earth, the one thing none of us finds easy to forsake. How did Jesus do it, when he of all people knew its satisfaction? How did he say no to Satan, not once but three times?

Forty days—a special period. The flood lasted forty days. Jesus' temptation lasted forty days. Lent lasts forty days: forty days to prepare, to repent, to purge our souls of all that is not holy. We have forty days to ready ourselves to walk the way of the cross with our Lord, but it is not long enough with all we must do.

I don't want four days or even four hours of sacrifice. How can I bear forty days? Forty days of saying no to myself and yes to others? Not when I've spent forty years saying—and doing—the opposite. How can I hope to learn the lesson Lent teaches in so short a time?

When I read the account of Jesus' temptation, I hear a man of utter commitment and single-mindedness. How firmly he tells Satan to remove himself. Jesus never hesitates, never hems and haws, never wonders whether compromise is possible. He knows the fundamental choices of life. *If only I could be like that. Well, I can't, so why should I bother?* No, Jesus could teach me how, a lesson at a time, no matter how slow a learner I am.

H e can teach me the lessons of sacrifice, giving up, ashes, doing what I don't want to do because it's the right thing to do. Seventh-graders are only just beginning to put life's pieces together. It's hard enough for them to see the principles behind grammar or algebraic formulas, but the principles of life? Many adults never understand the losing life/finding life principle, the ashes to ashes way of living. It's hard for us to believe that by giving up something we want we may end up with something much greater than we ever imagined. The grace of God gives such things to us; the grace of God helps us sacrifice.

February can be a hard month of lessons. Christ's impending death faces us daily, as it did him. Ash Wednesday reminds us of our sin and Christ's sinlessness— until the cross. The physical agony of his death was insignificant compared to his spiritual agony. Did he feel the black rot of evil eating away at his soul, creeping into his lungs and heart, down his legs, through his bloodstream until it reached his kidneys, pancreas, and liver? Corruption. Could he smell it? Could he taste it?

All of this is Ash Wednesday, when we should gladly relinquish a place we want, a food or a habit we love. Perhaps Protestants are uncomfortable with Ash Wednesday because it follows Mardi Gras, an excuse for debauchery, evidence that we can twist anything meant to better us into something to titillate us. But Ash Wednesday also follows Shrove Tuesday, the day for confession, the day of soul-searching to discover what it is that needs to go.

There are times when a Lenten sacrifice should never end. Forty days without backbiting, forty days without complaining, forty days of cheerful giving should become forty weeks, forty months, forty years, forty lives. But there's a risk of turning Ash Wednesday and Lent into spiritual hauteur. Suddenly, we are better than

someone without the willpower to sacrifice what we
have. Then, sacrifice sours in the mouth. A person who
humbly tries and fails has achieved greater spiritual
maturity.

Is my Ash Wednesday attitude an attempt to make
myself worthy of Christ's coming sacrifice? Yes. And no.
Christ carries his cross regardless of my worth. Yet he
loves me, nonetheless. I'm unworthy, too, of my
mother's love or my husband's love or the love of anybody else dear to me. But because I love them and am
conscious of my unworthiness, I try to strengthen my
shoulders with rigorous spiritual exercise—of sacrifice,
of humility, of giving—to bear their mantle of love, which
shimmers with color and ripples with texture; anyone
who wears such a mantle will sometimes stumble under
its weight. My attempts to make myself lovely for God
may be feeble, even laughable, but my motive is right.

So each Lent finds me wondering what I'll sacrifice,
what image will rule my attempt to wash my face and
comb my hair for God. This year I decided on a taste I
love, on a substance I've craved since childhood, a crystal
that has made nations rich and others poor: salt. I gave
it up because I love it. I ate to taste salt—the only taste
I wanted was salt. Salt was a kind of idol that I
rationalized into acceptability.

Daniel Boorstin explains the importance of salt to the
economy of the Middle Ages. Countries that abounded
in salt were prosperous, stable lands. People who used
salt freely were the aristocrats, the rulers. The poor
guarded it, hoarded it, shook it parsimoniously on food.
Without salt, some people had no food, since it preserved
meat and often hid the taste of rancid victuals. Salt enhanced and preserved life. Countries that lacked it sent
explorers to find it.

Salt is one of those substances that can be good or
bad—it depends how we use it. Our bodies require a

certain amount of sodium, some more than others. When my parents or friends complained about the amount of salt I used, I rationalized that my body needed a little extra—well, a lot extra—sodium. Because my blood pressure is quite low, I claimed that without all the salt I consumed, I wouldn't have *any* blood pressure. Nevertheless, I consumed enough salt to injure most people.

I was wasting it. Jesus used salt as a metaphor for our vocation in life, yet in my life it had become an image of sin. He said we're to be the salt of the earth. We think of someone who is bedrock solid, root-like, foundational, the quidity of an ordinary person, society's fundamentalist. That's not bad, but not quite what Jesus meant. We're to be the wealth of creation, the preservers and cleansers, those who invigorate the land. Jesus will use us judiciously, and we are to use ourselves judiciously, to salt the earth.

Those of us who have eaten salt-free bread know how bland it can be. Only a few teaspoons or a tablespoon of salt to four or more cups of flour is all bread needs for flavor. With too much salt bread is inedible. It's possible to have too much of a good thing.

Some of us good saltshakers are giving our communities too much; we need to sacrifice our saltshaking. Others of us are hoarding salt as the wealthy and powerful did in the Middle Ages; we need to give away our salt, another kind of sacrifice. How difficult to be a balanced metaphor. A little salt and the tastebuds of our neighbors might twitch and prickle at the tang of God's grace, their appetites enhanced for more, their noses sniffing the air for another whiff of that delightful scent. Too much and we deaden their tastebuds or overload their olfactory glands. Some of us may have lost our savor entirely, something Jesus warns about. So we salt and salt, without effect. Jesus knew that once salt becomes flat, no amount of salting the salt will bring back its savor.

F ebruary could use some salting, that's for sure. In the North it drags its muddy feet in and out, no matter how you beg February to wipe them at the door. Mud and slush everywhere. Windows cloudy with soot, walls and rugs and draperies hung over with the evidences of an oil-burning furnace. And then the flu is always lurking around some corner. Not even Ash Wednesday or the purification of sacrifice can deter the flu if it's determined to visit. February itself is a kind of flu—an achy, dreary, coughy, sniffly, sneezy kind of time. The most I usually hope with February is to endure it. If there's ice and I can skate, February redeems itself. Why must the beginning of Lent so often fall in February? To give up salt *and* live with frumpy February is asking too much. I used to fumble through this month with the worst possible case of flu. This happened five years in a row—minimum of three weeks in bed. I decided my climate was wrong. Not cold enough to make those germs hibernate, yet too cold to pretend it was March or April. So I moved north.

People here, Michiganders or Michiganians (both terms sound animal-like, a new species of caribou goose, or something), give February the slip by heading south. We decided to beat February at its own game; we headed even farther north.

A prehistoric fish, one without fins or scales, still exists in certain of our lakes and rivers. Rare now, this fish was a mainstay of the Indians in Ottawa, Kent, Berry, and Allegan counties here in West Michigan in the 1800s. The fish is large; in this state today anything under fifty inches cannot be kept. Wisconsin has even stricter rules. The sturgeon—ugly, slow, muscular—has an enormous mouth and a body covered by plates. Today, fishermen catch the biggest sturgeon out West, in the Columbia River, for example. But they can still take good-sized sturgeon in northern Michigan; during one month of the year, February, spearing sturgeon is legal.

A friend of ours, an outdoorsman and hunter, suggested that we give February a miss and head up to Black Lake for a day to try our hand at spearing sturgeon. It appealed to me. If February was miserable in western Michigan, we'd go where it was even more miserable and then brag we'd survived. It's almost the only thing a person living in the North in February has left to him: his ability to endure without complaining.

And maybe we'd land some fish.

Fishing for sturgeon involves waiting more than fishing. You sit, hoping that the fish will come to you. Although ice-fishing is normally a cold occupation, we rented a heated shanty for the day, complete with a large three-by-six-foot hole in the ice, a decoy that slowly unwound under water on a long cord attached to the roof of the shanty, and a twenty-five pound spear. Because I couldn't even lift the spear, my only job was to take turns watching for a fish. The rotating decoy quickly mesmerized us. We couldn't believe that the bottom of the lake was twenty feet away.

The only light in the heated shanty came from the water itself. (Light hurts the ability to see dark moving objects under the water.) The job sounds easy—just stare at a cold pool of water until a fish swims in sight. So we sat there all day. Did we see a small fish swim along the edge of the ice? We weren't sure. What a strange way to escape February.

It's probably a good thing we never saw a sturgeon because we had no way to practice heaving the spear into the water. A spear muddies the sandy-bottomed water for at least two hours afterward; a fish could enter and leave an ice hole without us knowing it. Throwing the spear with enough force, even for a large man, would be difficult enough, but he must also compensate for the refraction of the water. A person could so misjudge a fish's location as to miss the fish entirely. For an inexperienced spearman the only practice comes with the chance to hit or miss a fish. I'm amazed at the skill it takes; yet that was the principal way the Indians fished.

If nothing else, waiting for sturgeon exercises a person's patience and concentration. We met a man who had waited eighteen years to spear his first sturgeon. And he was none too proud of himself: "It was only a small one," he said apologetically. He hung his head as he said it, afraid that we'd recognize him another time and point to him mockingly as the man who waited eighteen years for a small one, an unworthy one.

That day was one of the only times I recall doing absolutely nothing, except eating an occasional apple. I couldn't even read—too dark—a self-imposed retreat into silence, my strange version of a Catholic spiritual retreat and following fast on the day of ashes. All sorts of relevant and irrelevant questions came to my mind as I sat dark and quiet: *What am I doing here? Why am I doing this? How much of this could a person take? Wouldn't a hair shirt have been easier?*

Not being used to this kind of retreat, I let my mind wander. A true spiritual retreat would have had some purpose. Yet I left that hut feeling as relaxed as I had in years. For a few hours, I had sacrificed every activity; now I was prepared to reenter the world.

Ashes in the snow, melting the cold, warming the soul, marking the body for God. Not a hair shirt, as sacrificial as wearing one would be. Not a permanent retreat into silence, as some medievals were driven to attempt. But ashes once a year, insistently reminding us of what real sacrifice means, holding up for us an example we cannot escape, before which silence and inactivity are the only responses. Once we've seen the ashes and listened to the darkness, we can never make more of our sacrifices than we should. What's a few hours for someone we love or a few dollars for someone in need, compared to those ashes, those death wounds. Silent sturgeon fishing put me in perspective. I am not so small as I would like to brag in impious humility; nor am I so large as my eyes see me. And that, of course, is the point of the sacrifice, the necessity of the ashes.

6   March Confession

I always go a little mad in March. February is over, reason enough for madness. I'm not made of the stuff of rigorous monastics. The life of hair shirts and ashes, though absolutely necessary at times, does not rest easily on my frame. Oh, it's still Lent. I continue with my giving-up discipline—though by now I'm used to it, so I suspect it's lost its effect. Refusing salt is now habit. I should have several things ready to relinquish; once the first sacrifice no longer is efficacious, I could lunge at the next sacrifice on my list. That sounds suspiciously similar to the way spiritual maturity should progress in any season. But as for Lent, I only have two things on my list. I now relinquish them without a twinge.

March is another month closer to spring. In some parts of the country, March is spring. It's taken me several years to forgive Michigan for not being Washington, D. C., in March or even in April. Because I've adjusted my expectations, March no longer frustrates me as much as it did, though the madness remains, often showing itself in my intense desire to clean—not the house but the yard. There is nothing uglier than a March lawn of dead leaves, brown grass, limbs, twigs, branches, the odd piece of paper. Not to mention the mud. In March we cannot safely walk on the grass for fear of sinking ankle deep in the thawing, soggy ground. Nor are there any colors— not in the sky, not on the ground. Crocuses won't bloom until April.

Every year about this time I begin to believe we really do have the ugliest yard I've seen. Then my madness takes over and I have a tremendous urge to take our yard in hand, giving it a shake and a scrub-up. Weak measures will not do; it needs the strong-mindedness of the steel gray-haired Latin teacher I remember from high school. So I pin up my hair and get to work.

I take the toughest rake I can find and I attack the grass first. Half-rotted leaves, shells of black walnuts squandered by the squirrels, branches driven desperate by March winds—I rake them all. I cart away debris, wheelbarrow full after wheelbarrow full, all the while thinking evil thoughts of those friends who *claimed* to want our black walnuts. These trees may be valuable, their nuts a delicacy, but I'd cut them down if my husband would let me. Not only are they messy in any season, they're supposedly poisonous to other plantings.

Next I cut back old perennials, pull away leaves caught in the branches of bushes, and redefine the edges of flower beds. As I do this, I look for a lump in the lawn, a green sprout or shoot to reassure myself that all my plants have not died and that soon I'll see the bright tints of spring flowers.

Yet, the colorless first day of spring, though it might not agree with the chronological calendar, does fit that of the Church. It is still Lent, after all, and I'm still to be repenting of my sins in preparation for Christ's great sacrifice and triumph over death. My soul still needs a greater spring cleaning than my yard.

I confess I'm not nearly as ruthless with myself as I am with my grass and shrubs. I know I've got cartloads of debris that ought to be placed in some spiritual compost heap to decay into friable fertilizer. If there are any new buds sprouting in my soul, they may find it difficult to grow through the weeds and decayed vegetation. It's not easy to take a stiff rake to myself. But if I won't learn during Lent, when will I?

None of us likes to root out anything growing in our souls. Even our weeds look good to us, if only because they are ours. Any weed is better than a bare spot. I've often wondered why certain plants appeal to me when others—dockweed, chickweed, quack grass, nettles—are repugnant. Why do we, almost instinctively, know a weed from a legitimate perennial? Why does rudbeckia (black-eyed Susan) belong in a country border but not dandelions? What makes a weed a weed? Its uncontroll-ableness? Its coarseness? Its inability to allow other plants to grow alongside it? Weeds will have their way. They will always put up new shoots unless we keep any top growth from reaching the sun; if we do, eventually the root system will die. But try it with a perennial whose roots are easily discouraged. A little yanking and the plant dies.

Weeds provide an endless source of frustration to gardeners; they are an endless tension-reliever too. After taking all our anger and irritation out on sixty feet of border, there's not a lot left for the people we live with. (Maybe that's why city dwellers have more ulcers and other psychosomatic illnesses than those of us in the country.) For one thing, we're just too physically tired to argue. After a day in the garden, breathing can be an effort. Gardening—physical or spiritual—can also bring clarity to problems; weeding and thinking go hand in hand. In fact, the more I weed, the clearer I see my need for cleaning and confession.

B ut you may not think the same way I do. Until recently, I assumed God had made everyone's brains more or less the same. Our circulatory systems function much alike, as do our hearts, lungs, livers, and so forth. But brain researchers have discovered that a person's brain is as individual as his features or his fingerprints. Scientists suspect that much of someone's personality is determined by the look of his brain: where his language ability is located, for example, or how well-developed is the intuitive area of his brain.

Scientists, having known for some time that the brains of men and women differ, suspect that language is more localized in men than in women and that women have a more developed area for fine motor skills. Scientists also know that the brains of right-handed and left-handed people differ considerably. It seems there are no ordinary people. God, of course, knew that all along, and I'm certain he despairs my ever learning it, no matter how many lessons he sends, no matter how much I confess my failure.

Yet we meet them every day—people we call ordinary, who seem to have few distinguishing features: the wallflower people. They seem to do nothing extraordinary: They have no interesting hobbies or habits, no unusual personality quirks. Or if they do, they face life with such a bland countenance that we don't bother to investigate them. All of us went to high school with such people. I did.

Ed Skilton was his name, though he called himself Tony. I didn't know him well; not many of us did. He was smart enough, but he wasn't much interested in school, which meant that he wasn't part of the "in" crowd. Actually, Tony wasn't in any crowd at all. He was poor, definitely from the wrong side of the tracks in that small Pennsylvania town. To superficial teenagers—and I was one—he wasn't worth noticing. No one disliked him—a pleasant kid with an offbeat sense of humor—but nothing more, mere background to the important people and events in my high school.

Tony had at least one close friend, Lance Craighead. Lance was not a wallflower. Although he may not have been as high socially as a football or basketball star, he was somebody to notice: son and nephew of the Craighead brothers, the leading experts in grizzly bears, then and now. He worked with his father and uncle each summer out West. Lance had been on television with his father and uncle; they had been published in *National Geographic*.

Tony and Lance were friends because they shared a love of the outdoors. In some vague way, I knew that Tony had a life quite different from that of the typical high schooler: He fished constantly. Tony was self-contained, assured, unconcerned that he was different. He wasn't withdrawn, just preoccupied with interests that didn't include us.

I haven't seen Tony since a chance summer encounter at a restaurant where I worked during college. He was earning his way through school writing short stories for such major publications as *Field and Stream* and *Outdoor Life*. Even then I knew that a person had to be good to be published in those magazines; college students usually weren't that good. Finally Tony had impressed me. What he didn't tell me was that he also paid his tuition by tying flies for trout fishermen. He was on his way to becoming one of the expert flytiers in the country, and, incidentally, one of the foremost fly-fishermen. I know why he didn't tell me. If he remembered anything about me, he knew I was an avid reader and that I just as avidly avoided anything that smacked of the out-of-doors. Back then, I wouldn't have known what tying flies meant.

Tony died recently. About a year ago, I received in the mail the names, addresses, and occupations of my high school class. As I glanced through it, Tony's name stood out: Director of the Orvis Fishing School in Vermont. It is the prestigious school of its kind in the country. Because we receive the Orvis newspaper, I learned that Tony died of cancer, lymphoma. The newspaper dedicated the last page to Tony, his personality, his accomplishments, his loving care of his wife and son Lance, his brilliance as a fly-fisherman. I was proud I had gone to school with him, yet humiliated that I had thought so little of him at the time. Tony's face became visible to me out of the background only because he did something I recognized as important, not because I saw God's extraordinary creation. Tony is no longer a nobody, but then he never was. It just took me twenty years to find it out.

Why do I learn so slowly? No matter how many times God shows me his grace and imagination in my fellow creatures, I still judge them by externals, still classify them as background or foreground people. God teaches me this lesson in so many ways—through Tony, through others who dazzle me with their instincts, wit, kindness, or self-sacrificing Lenten humility. I meet them every day. Not many of them are well-known; not many of them want to be. But they are amazing. Sue Dixon, a first-grade school teacher with an inventiveness and zeal for teaching people how to read, has developed a program to attack the growing illiteracy problem in our country. Robert Markham struggles to bear a painful burden, yet is always ready to help a friend. Darlyne Walker volunteers her time to help people learn. My list could go on and on; you have such a list, too. Most of us ignore these people, or take them for granted. We don't fuss over them; we don't give them the best seat. Their names don't have a media ring. But unimportant? Ordinary? No, these are the extraordinary people, the ones we should look to as examples. They've got the best seats reserved for them, and God booked their tickets.

Canadian writer L.M. Montgomery tells the story of a young girl named Emily, whose only desire is to become a writer. Because she has all the faults of the young romantic, her strict teacher tries to keep her from purple prose and overstatement by urging her to write simple character sketches of ordinary people, the people she knows. Emily answers him, "But there are no ordinary people." "Yes," muses her teacher, "but I wonder how *you* know that."

Whether we're talking about that high school student no one thought much of, or about the neighbor down the street who seems unremarkable at first glance, we're talking about extraordinary people. God can't make any other kind. Our brains, our physical structures, our personalities, our habits, our goodness are unique to us alone. Even our sins mark us individually. We share the need for confession and forgiveness, but not necessarily the specifics. We share the need to confess our mistreatment of one another, our degrading of God's human creations.

W hy do we no longer practice the regular discipline of confession? As with so many other good spiritual disciplines, we have abused and misunderstood it. We should have reformed the practice instead of dispensing with it altogether. Necessity forces us to consider our sins, especially those insignificant ones, which, just as with ordinary people, are probably the most important. The minor slight of another's feelings, a refusal to listen to our child, a dismissal of what our wife or husband needs, and why. No great sins. No adultery, murder, theft—but lots of pride, petty envy, minor jealousy, or lust. *The Book of Common Prayer* in its service of morning confession directs the congregation to pray, "forgive those things which we have left undone; forgive those things which we have done." Those two sentences cover every sin I possess. We easily recite the sins of commission, but the sins of omission? Confess something I haven't done? It sounds illogical, yet my soul's health depends on it.

How I love the litany of my accomplishments; how I detest the Lenten confession of the good I have failed to do. I squirm when asked "Why?" Why didn't you spend time with Greg and Allen? Why didn't you write your mother? Why didn't you call on your sick friend or bring a pot of soup to a neighbor with a broken arm? I know the excuse; I also know the reason. I was too busy; I was too selfish; I was too preoccupied. My book or my garden or my bath or my whatever was more important than another person. These are the confessional necessities of Lent. When we leave confession out of our services and ignore it in our daily and weekly prayers, we doom ourselves to spiritual inertia. We may enjoy our lack of confession for a while, but eventually its weight will drag us to a standstill.

Jesus began his ministry with purification, another kind of confession. He knew the proper order; he accepted the priorities. He was also, in so many ways, ordinary. We think of Jesus as charismatic, a combination Billy Graham, James Dobson, Chuck Swindoll, Billy Sunday, Pat Robertson, and probably a few other people we could name. Yet he was a nobody, a lowly itinerant preacher with a following of fervent disciples, an uneducated, country bumpkin from Nazareth who claimed to be God's son, the Messiah. He infuriated the Pharisees. If anybody should claim messiahship, it ought to be one of their crowd. How could a nobody lead the Jews against Rome?

God planned it well, of course. Most of us are nobodies, and Jesus came and died for us, not just for the wealthy, educated, highly articulate and highly visible spiritual leaders among us. (I hear Emily Dickinson whisper, "I'm nobody. Are you nobody, too?") His was a universal death, a death for all the background people in the world, as well as for those who condemn people to that status. Jesus showed how often God hides the extraordinary in the everyday, the ordinary, the nothing special. He does it with people like Tony; he does it with experiences. When God uses and transforms the routine, we shortchange ourselves—and him—waiting for the miraculous. We want something special, or we want nothing at all. This sin is deep-rooted dockweed. If Lent has any purpose, it should show us that there is no one beneath our notice.

A lthough March continues Lent, it also leads into spring. Soon we'll throw off the cloak of confession for the clothes of the Resurrection. And once the Resurrection occurs, summer returns, and with it life; death is defeated. Those gardeners who do not want to be behindhand in this seasonal resurrection should already have their seeds. The late Lenten season, just as Advent, is a time to prepare for life.

Because it takes planning to have a garden, last-minute people need not bother. Many gardeners go to the local garden shop and pick up a couple of tomato plants for a few dollars, though for less money than they spend, a person can have fifty or more. Walter Berry, poet, novelist, essayist, and Kentucky farmer, believes that we have so divorced ourselves from the land, from producing food for ourselves, that our values are skewed. We no longer understand nature's rhythms, which reinforce the spirit's rhythms: confession, death, resurrection. I have far greater respect and understanding today of what my produce store carries than I had before I grew my own vegetables.

So I spend a few dollars on seeds and reap hundreds of dollars of produce. I spend a few hours planting pepper, tomato, melon, cauliflower, and broccoli seeds in March to eat well in July, August, September, October, and beyond. But there's always a certain anxiety about gardening. Is this the year my pepper seeds won't sprout? Or my tomatoes?

Seed packets explain that seeds should sprout within seven to ten days, depending on conditions. That means temperature, humidity, moisture, quality of seed, and, I think, some old-fashioned luck. Some seed companies actually tell you the percentage of germination—85 percent germination, 70 percent. No one ever claims 100 percent. Yet after two weeks I still have no pepper seedlings. Maybe my house is too cold.

Each year I carefully plant my seeds in soilless seedling mix, properly dampened. Wetting the planting medium is the most time-consuming part of the job. Then I cover the damp soil and seeds with plastic. Although my seeds have always sprouted—eventually—for the first two weeks I hover over them anxiously. I never quite believe that a seed will suddenly become a plant, leaf at one end, root at the other. This year I was even more scientific. No more egg cartons covered by Glad Wrap. I bought the APS Self-Watering Plant System—a revolutionary new way to start seeds, a system designed in England. The reputation of English gardeners was enough to sell me, that and the fact that the planting containers are reusable.

The system looks great, quite professional. But I still don't have any pepper sprouts. I'm doubly disappointed because of what happened last year. My peppers sprouted beautifully, nice strong seedlings. I put them in the sunniest window I have, but left it open. A sudden early spring windstorm came up. I found my pepper plants on the floor, root balls bedraggled, stems and leaves limp. I might have saved them, but I was too disgusted; I threw them away.

Greg and I love peppers, green, red, yellow, or chocolate brown. We eat them in anything and everything. When making a salad Greg asks, "How many peppers can I put in?" I had looked forward to harvesting lots of them, using them in salads, soups, stews, chili. There seems to be no end to the use for peppers. Peppers are also good for you, especially the homegrown kind. When green, peppers contain moderate sources of vitamins A and C. Allow them to ripen to red and they increase in vitamin A, the vitamin researchers have found to be beneficial in preventing cancer.

Seeds are supposed to sprout—or die, another way of looking at the same process. Why won't mine? A seed has to stop being a seed to become a plant; all the seed catalogs tell you so, as do farmers, as did Jesus. He talked about all kinds of seeds—mustard seed, good seed, bad seed, seed properly planted, seed scattered at random, seed planted in rocky soil, seed planted in good soil. Jesus knew that no matter what, some seed just wouldn't act seed-like. They wouldn't die, even when he showed the way; See, he said, dying isn't so bad.

What obstinate seeds we are, determined to go our own way regardless of what our Creator intended. Since we don't know what's going to happen, we don't want to take any chances. Now if God would only show us a lush pepper plant and say, See how beautiful you will be, maybe we'd cooperate. But even then I have my doubts. I might decide that a stalk of corn is more to my liking than a pepper bush or a head of lettuce. Corn is taller, sweeter, juicier. I will be corn; I will not be ordinary onion, and this, too, must be confessed. What does a gardener do when his seeds don't know what's good for them?

G od gives us possibilities. Even during the dusty Lenten times, the March madness times, God shows us what we'll look like when he's done sprucing us up, when he gets the last bit of dockweed out of our souls. He gives us a lifetime of springs which we never outgrow. Spring comes at any time, in any place, during any circumstance, no matter how winter-like. God gives us a chance for spring when we see someone as God does, when we practice the disciplines of confessing, cleansing, and dying. Spring is a surprise, and it's a surprise every time, even when we're expecting it. If last year or the year before it was wet and cold, this year spring might be warm and dry. Each year the flowers behave differently; daffodils, flowering crab apples, and speireia match their floral display to the weather, if not always to the temperament of the beholder.

Spring knows no calendar. In Florida flowers bloom early, in New England, late. Weather that finds us still wearing winter coats has birds up and stirring in warmer areas. At thirty-five degrees the robins are off; spring peepers like it a little warmer, fifty degrees. What is the temperature when humans slough off their winter skin? Fifty? Sixty? My husband still wears a flannel shirt and wool sweater when it's seventy.

At thirty-five degrees the earth is warming, even if we aren't. Worms move to the surface, aerating the soil as they go. At forty-four degrees buds start to swell on trees and plants. Next spring take a look. Although we may still be running the furnace, noticing the buds makes us feel warmer for a lot less money. Once flower buds have opened, hummingbirds know their spring has come. Swallows pick up spring with the arrival of flying insects, honeybees with the production of pollen. Lots of us with allergies use that same measure to tell when spring has arrived; we have more in common with bees than we think.

No matter where we look in nature, spring makes a difference. Ocean tides peak in spring. Freshwater ponds and streams completely turn over, the water from the bottom coming to the top, the surface water moving down. Fish, as any fisherman knows, travel to shore to spawn. Babies born in spring are, on average, bigger than those born in other seasons. Even our blood chemistry changes slightly in spring. Perhaps the spring tonic of our grandparents' era wasn't such a bad idea.

Spring fever is common to all creation. God put something into spring that he left out in the other seasons. We need the rest of winter; but we also need our blood altered and our senses stirred when it ends. Each of us is struck by different things during March; no two people, just as no two creatures, respond exactly to the same stimulus. Some people can smell spring in the air as early as February. Others wait until the forsythia or dogwood bloom. Then, of course, there is opening day of baseball season, not this month, but soon, just a few more weeks of spring training until we hear those marvelous words, "Play ball." It's a time of endless optimism because we know that *this* year, after waiting all those years, our team will win. And it will start with those two euphonious words.

God gave us a marvelous gift when he created this wonderfully chaotic, seemingly haphazard time of year, a time for madness as well as a time for confession. He follows the same pattern in everything he does. A kind word at the end of a hard day or an encouraging word at the beginning of a long one brings soft breezes and the sweet scent of alyssum. A helping hand with a difficult task is as refreshing as a spring shower on out-stretched plants. An understanding attitude when understanding isn't easy can help bring out the blossom in another person.

It takes keen eyes and clear nostrils—the result of confession—to catch spring at the beginning, long before the rest of us are aware of it. Who doesn't know spring when the weather warms and the rhododendron and azalea replace forsythia and daffodil in the flower show? But to feel the earthworms moving and the earth warming at thirty-five degrees or to catch the breeze of a robin's wings and to see the buds swell at forty-four degrees takes perception most of us lack. Yet every day, no matter what the season, we have a chance to alter the blood chemistry—and the heart and respiration—of another person when we say, "Come on. You can do it. You're someone special." We can bring spring to those around us, if we watch, keen-eyed and clear-nosed, for our chance. We can even be altered ourselves.

I hope everyone is a little mad in spring; then no one will notice my madness. At least now I know that I have my overactive blood chemistry to blame.

7   April Exuberance

April and Easter, that movable feast, do not always come together, but in my calendar they do. Easter is the word we've been waiting for, the cool spring drink for which we've suffered through the dusty, throat-clogging spring cleaning of Lent. Of all words, the *yes* of Easter is the most welcome word we hear all year. It is our alleluia. But first, before we can hear the yes and shout the alleluia, we've got to learn to read the right words.

Sleep Cheap. Speed checked from air. Courtesy. Common Sense. Caution Curves. Have you checked your headlights? Visit the Football Hall of Fame. The wages of sin is death. Toledo 69 miles. Chicago 320 miles. Jesus Saves. Coke Is It.

Road signs. Billboards. What would God's signposts say? *I'll rebuild my temple in three days*?

Travel any highway and you'll see words. The billboard advertisers are counting on us reading fanatics to read them, every one. But after a few hundred miles, the story wears a little thin. My mind continues to read the roadsigns at the same time that it sings, "Words, words, words, I'm so sick of words. I get words all day through, first from him, now from you. Is that all you blighters can do?" Musical comedy fans will recognize those words from *My Fair Lady*, which introduced Pygmalion (and George Bernard Shaw) to millions of people. I sympathize with the sentiment of the song. Even a person addicted and absorbed by words sometimes needs a break from them. Of course, it never happens; even in sleep we dream with words. With all the words floating around, we ought to understand each other better. Why don't we?

Nothing is more difficult than being understood. You say a set of words, but I hear another. Novelists and comedians have a long-standing tradition of using this difficulty to great advantage. Does this situation sound familiar?

"When will dinner be ready? I'm starved," Steve shouted to Carole, his wife.

"In just a few minutes. We're waiting for the potatoes to finish cooking. The table needs to be set, and I'm making salad." Carole had had a long, hard day. All she wanted was to sit quietly, eat her dinner, and drink some iced tea. She was so thirsty. As she worked she thought of everything that had happened today. The top heating element in her oven had taken off in a convincing imitation of a firecracker and melted itself amid sparks and sound effects. Her sink had clogged up. Nicholas had been playing Noah and the Ark in the bathtub. They now had water spots on the ceiling below the bathroom. She'd wait till after dinner to let Steve know that. *Sometimes*, thought Carole, *I think we take Nicholas to church too much. What if he decides to reenact David and Goliath or Esther, or . . .*

"Do we have to wait for the potatoes? Can't we get started without them?" shouted Steve.

That was the last straw for Carole. There he sat, doing nothing, while she worked on dinner. Hadn't she asked him to set the table for her? He sounded like she was his personal short-order cook. How dare he accuse her of poor planning and inefficiency? She was hungry too. What was wrong with him? She'd just about had it with his attitude. Maybe he'd like to fix his own dinners from now on. "Now wait a minute, Steve—"

We'll leave them to fight it out. If Carole is at all persuasive in her use of words, and Steve at all sensible in how he understands them, all will be well. If not, it could be the first of many arguments or it may be the last the couple can tolerate. Words can be a real problem.

If I say, "I'll take care of this tomorrow," you may hear, "You're not interested in my problem." Tell ten-year-old Nicholas, "We'll have to think about that," and he thinks, *Great. Mom says I can do it.* Later, after his mother finally says a definite no, he may wail, "But you told me I could." To people who want to hear yes all the time, an affliction particularly prevalent among children, anything short of a flat no means yes. No matter what we do, we often cannot make ourselves understood. Nor can we understand others; words are too slippery, tone and body language too noisy.

Maybe that's why the Bible says to let our yes be yes, and our no be no. (Maybe that's why Easter moves around; we never know when we need a yes.) Sounds easy enough, but try it. Either people want elaborate explanations or we feel compelled to give them whether or not they're wanted. Although we want to justify, rationalize, and objectify why we say yes or no, most of the time we simply feel like saying yes or no. Growing up, I always thought my parents said no simply on whim;

it wouldn't do to say yes too often and set any precedent that might give me the upper hand. As with any child, I always wanted to know why: "because I said so" never satisfied me. (That's one of those things children determine never to say when they become a parent, and one of the first things we find ourselves saying when we are; sometimes it seems that life is packed with perversity.)

The word *why* is too ready to fall off our tongue. It may be as quick a word as yes or no, but certainly more difficult to avoid; the why questions are the ones we can't say yes or no to. Although we talk and talk and talk, we get no further ahead than if we said nothing. Whether we're trying to understand and be understood by our family or our co-workers or trying to understand and be understood by God, the job takes more effort and patience than most of us possess. Some days a hermitage is the only option that has any appeal, a vow of silence the only oath we want to utter.

When words frustrate me most, I try to look at them from God's perspective. He's had this communication problem with us from the start. He couldn't have been any clearer than when he said, "Don't touch that tree." Like a typical parent, though, he didn't tell us why, and that's the question the serpent used to trap Eve. He urged her to think about the question, to analyze what God really meant and to try to figure out his reasons. The serpent led Eve to the heart of the problem; surely God couldn't have meant what he said, not literally; no one ever does. Because we never want to believe that a person's word can be taken at face value, we search diligently for the unspoken agenda, listening harder to unspoken words than to spoken ones. We find it easier to listen to what someone hasn't said than to what he has. Other people may have unspoken agendas; God doesn't. His yes means yes, his no means no. How can we hope

to understand each other, when we persist in mis-
understanding God?

Clear, unadorned speech has power and beauty. Yet
because simplicity makes us nervous, we garnish it with
adjectives. "I'm a man" or "I'm a woman" is fare too
plain; we add handsome, smart, pretty, unique, quick-
witted, complex—all attempts to define ourselves and
each other. There's nothing wrong with definition. We
all need it. But when we start telling people only what
we think they want to hear, then we've passed from
letting our yes be yes and our no be no to something
very close to lying.

We're all guilty. We must be missing some ethical ingredient that tells us when we're lying, since we lie not
only to other people but also to ourselves when we promise something we can't possibly accomplish. Looking
good to others and to ourselves overrides our sensitivity
about the truth. We promise what we can't deliver; we
make people happy initially, only to disappoint them
later. Maybe we don't intend to lie. Maybe we think we
really can fit one more appointment into our already
crowded schedule. Maybe we think we will have the
money to buy our child what he wants or the time to
take him on the special trip he's been pleading for. Maybe
we really mean to save an evening just for our husband
or our wife. Then the time comes and we back out.
Although it's bad enough to do this to one another, we
also do this to God.

The hardest time of all to face our limitations is in the
spring. The feast of the Resurrection is upon us; Lent is
nearly done. With shoots of crocuses and daffodils, nature finally looks to be growing out of its winter gar-
ments. Although science may have told us that the buds
on the trees were already swelling, now we see them

clearly; daily they become larger and softer. Christ is freeing us from the bondage of the body. Surely we can conquer words if he can conquer death. Maybe.

Jesus is probably the only person to have used his yes and no correctly. *I'm going to death*, he said, a yes statement. *I will rise again*, another yes statement. *I refuse to be tempted*, he said to Satan, a no statement. *I will send a comforter*, he told his disciples, another yes statement. When Jesus said something, it stuck, and he stuck to it. He enjoyed the full range of living because he knew the importance of *meaning* those two small words. All our relationships depend on them. *Yes, I'll call*—and then do so. *Yes, I'll go to the store for you. No, I won't leave you. No, I won't stop loving you*—or to put it positively, *Yes, I'll always love you, no matter what*. That's the statement on which too many of us stub our toes.

True yes living marks Easter, our spiritual spring. We don't want to see Christ rise as we hold a bunch of meaningless yeses, garlanded with a bouquet of nos. Rather, we want to sniff and feel the exuberance of youth, the exuberance of the body made new, the exuberance of a sparkling season. April, though marching toward us, will turn aside if it reaches someone too overburdened to open his arms to the charms of early childhood, of fish on the beach, of the verbs *splash* and *squish*.

The April of Easter offers such exuberance to all of us, young and old. Exuberance means more to those of us old enough to recognize it. Unfortunately, children have no consciousness that theirs is an exuberant time. Because they know nothing else, they don't need to think about it. Only later do we remember how exuberant we were as children, even without a reason. When Easter splashes us with the joy of life, we never stop to ask Why? or Will it last? or What will happen when this ends? Because such times occur less frequently as we grow older—perhaps because we're too cautious—we remember them all the more poignantly.

I clearly recall such a time; I was nineteen. Stephanie was finishing her junior year in high school; I had concluded five straight semesters in college. One Sunday we drove around the Pennsylvania countryside near where we lived for no particular reason other than to drive around the country. (Who worried about gas consumption in those days?) Our family had decided to move to Maryland, just outside Washington, D. C. We weren't particularly sad about leaving the Cumberland Valley; none of us had ever liked it much. But it represented seven years of our short life, so perhaps Stephanie and I were unconsciously saying farewell.

That late spring day, because of the weather, because we saw the country as itself for the first time, we saw beauty everywhere. We rolled down the car windows and turned up the radio. Because we could not contain the exuberance we felt at moving, changing, growing up, remembering the past, anticipating the future, we sang every song we heard as loud as we could. This joy was rolled into an intense few hours. We were leaving behind a major part of our lives to begin the next era, which beckoned and beguiled us. After that day, we were never the same.

I don't know if everyone experiences a time when he knows, absolutely and unswervingly, that he will be different an hour hence (I don't mean such obvious changes as marriage); Stephanie and I knew, and we were right. Moving to Maryland forever changed the pattern of our lives, forever changed what would have been into what became.

Would the day and time have had the same impact on us had it not been balmy blue? I doubt it. Although exuberance can come in winter—or any season—April is the youngest time of year, and it holds the prerogative. The atmospheric conditions are never so ripe. Jesus' resurrection did not accidentally occur in the spring. What greater exuberance could there be than the first time a man rose from the dead? That's youngness in the extreme. No doubt the apostles suddenly saw their futures as much more beguiling than they had just a few hours earlier. A day, a few minutes, can make all the difference. It did in this case; the disciples, who were never the same after the women told them Jesus was alive, made sure that the world itself was changed.

What if we had been there when Easter began? People living under Roman occupation dreaded death just as much as we do. It takes a lifetime to believe in death. Only after watching plants die, animals die, and finally people die, can we believe in it—a little. Because life grips us so tightly, the hardest death to believe in is our own. The disciples faced their own death when they faced their Lord's. How impossible it was for them—and how impossible for us—to believe that someone had the cure. How angry and disappointed they would be if it turned out to be hokum. But if Jesus were alive, why then, so were they. So are we. Every inch the daffodils grow in April declares that Christ, the disciples, and we, are alive.

S pring may not be the time to think of death, yet the yarns of life and death cannot be unraveled without destroying the whole. Jesus had to die before he could live; first Good Friday, then the Resurrection. It's as true today as it was in the first century. Death surrounds us in the life swell of plants and seeds.

Early that spring morning I awoke, startled. Rolling over on my back, I lifted my arm to scratch my face, an act I've done without thinking since birth, I suppose. I knew where my face itched; my brain sent a message to my shoulder, arm, right hand, and, finally, fingers, first and second ones. They didn't respond. Somehow my two fingers were twisted, my right hand erratic. I completely missed the spot my brain had told my hand and fingers to hit; instead they brushed my nose. Again, without consciously thinking, I reached over with my left hand and made my right fingers do what they refused to do automatically.

Suddenly, I realized what I had done. My right hand and fingers wouldn't work. *A fluke*, I thought. *My imagination*, I reasoned. *Don't be ridiculous*, I lectured myself. My hand had to work. It *always* had worked. Why would it suddenly stop working?

Only a few seconds had passed since something had awakened me. *A bullfrog? An owl?*

Still not believing it, I gave my right hand another chance to prove me wrong. Again I raised my arm and moved it close to my face. *Scratch it*, I urged my hand. *Open*, I commanded my fingers. *Bend your knuckles*. And again, nothing but a spastic movement, uncoordinated, awkward, irrational. Again, I reached over with my domineering left hand to insist my right hand obey.

By now I was starting to panic. My heart was beating rapidly, my pulse racing, my body sweating. What was wrong? Still half asleep, I turned over on my left side, stretched my right hand onto the sheets, and using my left hand, slowly opened my fingers until they were flat against the bed. I pressed them downward. *Somehow, I* thought, *if I only leave them flat, the wrinkles will disappear and they will return to normal. But what if they don't? What if something is wrong with me? What would I do if my right hand is paralyzed? What will I tell Allen?*

As I tried to calm myself, I noticed for the first time a familiar tingling sensation in my forearm. Pins and needles, the British call it. *Maybe that's what had awakened me, not a bullfrog after all.* My arm had gone to sleep. My right hand and fingers couldn't work: no blood, no circulation, no feeling.

Although I knew what had happened, I was still afraid. I had moved quickly from a paralyzed hand to paralyzed legs, from walking to a wheelchair. No more running, or gardening, or cooking, or writing: everything gone that made life what it was for me. I was dizzy with relief that my fears were unfounded, angry that I had panicked so quickly. My body isn't supposed to matter so much.

Yet it does. So does yours. It did for Jesus; it did for the disciples and especially for Thomas, who didn't want to believe in the cure until he saw it for himself. No matter how much we spiritualize ourselves, we're still physical creatures. Although Jesus didn't want the pain of the cross, he carried it because he knew the cure would come no other way. He knew that death was the necessary prelude to life. I was physically nauseated at the thought of paralysis. Until we can't move, we don't think about the wonder of movement. How my eighty-nine-year-old grandmother, who can move with a walker but spends most of her time in her room, longs to move as she once could.

"Take up your bed and walk," Jesus said. To others, he said, "See" or "Speak." Did those commands mean more to the cripple than "Your sins are forgiven?" Jesus knew that "Be healed" included the unspoken words "I forgive you because you trust me." Did he know that his risen body would be more important to us than the doctrine of atonement? Easter celebrates the body. Christ sloughs off death like a blanket; he walks, eats, runs, fishes. His death, though the gateway to life, means nothing without his newly raised body. We want to be healed; we want to be raised from the dead; we want to be free from wheelchairs and braces and untimely fears that our bodies are dying. How do we know our sins are forgiven? The same way the cripple did. By taking up our bed. By walking. By running. By turning cartwheels and skipping rope. By hauling in the big one that didn't get away. Jesus loves our bodies, and he's going to give them back to us, better than new.

S o many exciting and blood-stirring spring exuberances reflect the joy of the body, of the Resurrection. The Resurrection provides the gloss and sheen to the rest. As people of ordinary events, though, a daily dose of Resurrections would overwhelm us, perhaps even frighten us. How Jesus' miracles disturbed people; he never left the ordinary alone. We have an amazing capacity—probably our emotional regulator—to function even in the most unusual circumstances, as if nothing unusual were happening. Joni Eareckson Tada experienced this on her wedding day—how extraordinary it was, and yet how ordinary it seemed to her.

What are some of my spring exuberances? First, we shout triumphantly, He is Risen. My blood, if not stirred before, is now heaving in my veins at the thought. I see color return to earth and fish jump in new-warmed water. But spring is also exuberant to me because it brings baseball, the most acutely theological, resurrection-like game I know. It is fitting that Easter and Opening Day come so close together.

The umpire shouts, Play ball, and we do. The count runs to three and two. You're out. Safe. A home run. Holy Cow. Sentence fragments they may be, but for any baseball fan they pack paragraphs. They conjure up a day at the park, when nutrition is forgotten; hot dogs, pizza, pretzels, and soft drinks reign supreme. Who would miss batting practice, even if it means rising early to reach Wrigley Field ahead of everyone else? Heading for the park at any time is exciting, but Opening Day can't be beat.

This day holds all the possibilities of the season. The Cubs may do it this year; they may go all the way. In 1984 when they won their division they almost did. On Opening Day every team stands equal, spring training notwithstanding. I'm always suspicious of teams that win in February or March. Should we win during Lent, or should we be learning how to lose? Come April, will those winners have anything left? The Tigers had an exceptional 1986 spring training: dead last, midway through the season. In baseball, it just doesn't pay to practice well; you've got to play well. It's the fundamentals that count, whether on the field or in the pew.

Baseball is like no other game we have. Space and time do not contain it. In football, soccer, or basketball, a ball out of bounds stops the play. In baseball there are no bounds to be out of. A foul ball is part of the game; breaking the bounds can bring one run or four. And no matter how many people say they want a pitching duel, home runs bring people to the park day after day.

In other sports the clock controls the game, but not in baseball. An inning can take five minutes or twenty-five minutes. A game may last three, four, five, even six hours; and some have. Theoretically, a tied game could last forever. Baseball renders time impotent. The teams play until one of them wins.

Stepping into the park on Opening Day or the last day of the season is stepping into eternity. It's the only time on earth when everyone in the park becomes a little child again. I've never seen a misbehaved child at a baseball game; no child would spoil so glorious an event. To appreciate baseball, a childlike spirit must prevail. Isn't this similar to the spirit Christ wants us to have, the spirit in which we embrace the Resurrection, grateful for the simple, gracious gift of life? We know we can surmount impossibilities; we know our team can come back in the bottom of the ninth no matter how many runs behind. The possibility of extra innings always excites us, and eternity lurks right down the left field foul line, just fair, and into the corner: eternity a sure triple, the most difficult hit to get.

Opening Day is the way to start the Resurrection—jogging, running laps, stretching muscles, retraining the eye, the mental and physical timing it takes to play ball. Of course, before the players take the field they've jogged and stretched their way through weeks of spring training. God has taken care of spiritual spring training with Lent and Easter, but remember: Easter is a physical feast as well as a spiritual one. We may be waiting for our resurrection bodies, but some of us have refused to keep our original bodies in shape. We violate the Easter feast when we make our hearts work too hard and our muscles work too little. We're doing everything wrong and wonder why we're so tired.

Because Easter celebrates the body, shouldn't we pay a little more attention to it than we do? I don't mean clothing and perfuming it better, just taking better care of the bones and sinews God gave us. I can't ever conjure up a picture of Jesus as overweight, sloppy, or out of breath. He needed every breath he had. Jesus knew just how strenuous his road would be. He knew when to say yes; he knew when to say no. He knew which exercises he needed. Jesus, more than anyone, worked under stress, but did it ever bother him? I doubt it. He had enemies wherever he went, an image to maintain, people always clamoring for another miracle. Golgotha was straight ahead, a cross to carry. Yet through it all, Jesus walked serene. He said what he needed, rested and played when necessary. He was in training for the greatest game of all, but he knew the unbeatable combination—prayer for the spirit, exercise for the body. Without those two, would he have seen Easter? Would we?

8 May Gardens, May Delights

O nce upon a time, a long time ago, there was a garden, lush, colorful, cool. Treemor discovered it quite by accident, the way so many of us do. He and his sister, Nella, were playing near the old fence in the back pasture where Grandpa Grendor just grazes a few sheep.

Their grandmother, Hilla, had excused them from chores, which surprised them. Their adventure began, said Treemor, as soon as they hit the first big rock, the one that's like home base when you play jump-the-rock. They were looking around for the sheep but didn't see any at first, which was strange. By the time they hit their third or fourth rock—Nella and Treemor disagreed here and never would get it straight—they noticed a little, unfamiliar gate. They only saw it then because a sheep was just the other side of it.

The sight of that sheep, seemingly so intelligent and not like a sheep at all, made Nella jump to the ground and run over to the gate, almost before she knew what she was doing.

"Nella, where are you going? Wait. Don't leave me behind. Hey, where'd you go? Nella!" Treemor shouted.

When he got over the gate, he looked around for a second and still couldn't see her. Then he noticed that the land took a kind of dip; maybe she was below him, out of his line of sight. So he started walking and calling her name. He soon heard a faint response.

"Treemor. Treemor. Come this way, to your left a little. Follow the bluebells. Follow the sheep. Follow the path. I've found the most beautiful garden." And so she had. By the sounds of it, she wasn't making up any tall tales when she said it was the most beautiful she'd seen. Later, she tried to show me where it was, claimed it reminded her of the garden in the Bible, but we never could find the entrance.

When Treemor finally found her, Nella was sitting in the midst of a bed of peonies, just sniffing and smiling.

"Are you about to cry or something?" Treemor asked, a little out of breath because he'd run the last bit.

"No, Tree. Why would I cry *here*? Isn't it something? I'm smelling the flowers. I tried each one and they don't smell like anything, but when I just sit here and sniff I can smell them all, each one separately and each one all together. Can't you smell it? Maybe you're too high. Come sit beside me."

Treemor obeyed, though why a person would want to sit and sniff was beyond him. "Isn't it almost like tasting the ripest strawberry on the hottest June day, Tree?" He had to admit it made his nose feel pretty good.

"Tree, look at all these beds. Someone smart planted these. A peony bed. A lilac border. Over there are some rhododendrons and azaleas with some solomon's seal close to those hostas. Look over to your left, beyond the crab apples. See those flowers in bloom? Those are mums and helenium. Then that little rock garden with the stream trickling through it. Those are all early spring flowers blooming. How did the gardener get them to bloom all at once? Spring and midsummer and fall flowers. They're all where they belong but all blooming at once."

While Nella was lost in flowers, Tree got a little restless, so he wandered off. Said he smelled water. That Tree can't resist putting a line in anything wet. A sheep or two followed along as a matter of course. Tree told me later that the path seemed to twist itself while he walked on it, like it was experimenting with being crooked. That path could have been playing or it could have been acting malicious-like, trying to throw Tree down. He never knew for certain which it was because just as the path took its last violent lunge, he found what he was looking for. "The sweetest little stream I've ever seen," he told us later, "and me with no pole and no bait."

Now when it comes to fishing Tree doesn't give up easy. "I looked around for a tree branch to break off, something quick to use for a pole. I could see the fish starting to rise, and I wanted them to rise for me. I had some string and a few hooks in my pocket, of course, so that was no problem."

Tree solved the bait problem by catching some grasshoppers and a dragon fly or two that happened along. Before he knew it, he'd caught six beauties. Used a nearby vine to string 'em with. "But then," Tree said, explaining why he and Nella had been gone the whole live-long day, "my troubles began. I started through the woods to look for Nella because I didn't know what else to do. But the more I walked the colder and meaner everything got. Frost seemed to be coming up through the garden and the leaves changed from fresh to brittle. I could tell by the sound. I thought about throwing the fish back in the water but couldn't bring myself to do it."

I wasn't sure I believed Tree's story. Not that he was lying, but he's read too many books about furry creatures who smoke and have adventures. He's always wanting adventures himself. I say it's adventure enough just to get up and do your duty by your place and your people. But if he was close to telling what really happened, maybe he's had enough adventures to last him a while.

Tree walked and walked, trying to find a way through the woods. Just when he thought he'd found the path, it would disappear or a vine or a sycamore would step in front of him.

"After a pretty long while, I knew I wasn't going to get through there. I had trees lined up in front of me like a wall, or a group of very determined soldiers," Tree continued. "So, I decided to go back to the stream, if I could find that. As I turned around, there was the path, rippling in places, but definitely headed back. I thought it was laughing at me."

While Nella and Treemor were out, a sudden late storm came up. Hilla didn't seem worried, not at first anyway. But the sky got darker and the storm stronger, and still no children. I told Hilla not even my old yellow slicker would keep out the rain; if she thought I was going up there to find them, she could just keep her thoughts quietly to herself. I had done my duty today and now it was my turn to rest a minute.

"They've got refuge," was all Hilla would say. Humph. How does she know these things? Because, of course they did. They didn't even know there was a storm.

As it was clearing, Nella and Treemor plodded up the walk, as dry as when they left that morning. "How'd you miss that storm?" I shouted out to them. They looked at each other, puzzled. I forgot to be irritated, though, when they started their story. I didn't want to believe it; maybe I still don't, at least not all the parts. Yet I wanted to go there. *Seems like I've always wanted to go there.* Or maybe I'd been there, once, a long time before, when I was young. Have you?

G od created a garden. And ever since we've been trying to get back there or recreate his efforts, but with what problems. God didn't face unknown or unseen insects that shoot holes through tender daisies or gaillardia. His moles undoubtedly behaved themselves much better than mine do. When God rooted a chrysanthemum, it came up the color it was supposed to. He never fenced in his corn or spinach. Nor did his sheep need the latest pens to keep them where they belonged. Walls and rock gardens proved no problem to him; they were level without much effort. Unsightly elms, dying of disease, certainly never plagued him.

God created a garden. Why can't we?

Even the simplest plants can prove intractable. Anyone can grow beans—provided he doesn't have an unexpectedly late frost or flooding. The black-eyed Susans I planted—a wildflower in Connecticut where I grew up— have taken several years to put on a show. Last year my gaillardia flowered from spring until frost. This year, nothing. Peas were prolific last year, this year pathetic. For every minor success, we have a major disaster. Too little rain. Well, we can always water. Too much rain. How can we get rid of it? For five years we had drought; then we had floods.

We don't have enough compost, either. It takes a long time to get a good compost pile going, no matter what the gardening articles say, and this is only our second year. Oh, no, too much fertilizer. How was I to know that peonies, alone in the plant kingdom, detest fertilizer and sulk if there's even a stray blade of grass near them? And yet delphinium pout without heaps of manure.

God created a garden. Adam and Eve had nominal upkeep to do—but I just can't imagine what it might have been. I know Milton thought they had work to do, but what kind? Certainly no weeding. The soil would hardly have been depleted, so they didn't need fertilizer.

The mists took care of the water problem. Were there insects in Eden? Or did the scent of marigolds, strong from creation, really keep pests away from cabbage and broccoli? Maybe plants grew so rapidly that Adam and Eve spent time dividing plants; yet many plants don't like to be split. Maybe they were learning how to rotate crops and husband the land.

When Adam and Eve sinned, they forever ruined my gardening. No matter what I do, I just can't overcome their initial act. God created a garden. I just hope heaven has a few bare spots for us frustrated gardeners because I've got some ideas.

I think Adam and Eve's sin also affected the animals— unless God created them troublesome. We all know how persnickety cats can be. One day they like kidney in cream gravy and the next they snub their noses at anything less than seafood supper. But we have animals—possums, raccoons, and rabbits—around our place who even out-discriminate cats. In the winter we've had rabbits attack our burning bush and dwarf sargent crab apple tree but ignore the cottoneaster, which they are supposed to love. This spring, they, or some other creatures, almost ate right through some young lilacs. I know God never had that problem.

The first year we had a vegetable garden, we planted three kinds of tomatoes, each kind in its own row (I've since given up being so systematic; the tomatoes don't care). I went out one morning to see if the early tomatoes were ready to pick, but something had been there before me. Every tomato plant had been picked clean, as if by human hands. The longkeeping tomatoes and the beefsteaks were untouched and remained untouched throughout the rest of the season. Possums, we eventually decided, had eaten all the early tomatoes, apparently the only ones they liked.

We also planted three kinds of corn: early sunglow, honey and cream, and silver queen. The raccoons took a fancy to the honey and cream. In one night they stripped every plant clean, just at its ripest. That's real discrimination. Picking the perfectly ripe ear of corn is no easy task.

Although I'm not against sharing my space with a few animals, I don't see why they have to choose my food to eat when the vegetation all around us is so lush. After a few years of this, Allen and I decided to do something about the problem; we put up an electric fence, a new variety developed for sheep farms in New Zealand. This handsome fence is as simple to string as, well, string. It runs on six large flashlight batteries. After putting it up, we turned it on. Nothing happened—no current, no big moment. We checked the batteries to make sure the contact was good and that they were in correctly. They seemed to be. When Allen tried it again, I was holding the fence with my left hand. "It works!" I shouted, jumping back several feet. An hour later I could still feel the current hitting my arm.

The instructions assured us that the charge wouldn't harm animals, just train them to stay away from the vegetables. I know it trained me. But because animals, unlike people, are not so easily discouraged, I wonder if the fence will really solve this problem. Again, I doff my gardening hat in Adam and Eve's direction. I hope they're satisfied.

Around here, late spring may be the time for planting gardens and putting up fences, but it's a time for other chores too: weeding, for example, or mowing the lawn, almost every day it seems. It's also the time to enjoy creeping phlox, candytuft, aubretia, and the other marvelous, it's-nearly-summertime plants. But it is not the time for death. Didn't Christ take care of that last month with the Resurrection? Although the last thing I want to see is anything dead, with a cat death comes anytime.

Lots of people, I know, don't like cats. Maybe because my mother grew up on a dairy farm and always had lots of barn cats—twenty or thirty—she always kept a few cats when I was growing up. For me, the question of liking cats is irrelevant. They're just part of my life, a necessity like washing my hair or doing the dishes. Although we only have one cat, Chesterfield, occasionally I've suggested getting one or two more. Allen, though, is monogamous, so we stick with Chesterfield.

Our cat fits his name. He weighs almost fourteen pounds, is solid gray, dignified most of the time, and a superb hunter. This is a converted cat—converted from city life to country ways. Born and raised in Manhattan, he never saw a tree or bush until he was well into adulthood. At first, even when he had the opportunity, he refused to venture outside. But slowly, Michigan's animal population tempted him. Now he's more an outdoor cat than an indoor one; once he discovered his prowess as a hunter he never looked back. Chesterfield has had to overcome some handicaps, though: no front claws and few teeth.

We never know when the cat will strike. Neither do the wildlife around our house. He has caught rabbits and squirrels nearly his size. Birds are no problem for him, nor are young opossum, or frogs, for that matter. I've watched him. Chesterfield seems so nonchalant, so carefree, so totally innocent, until, suddenly, he's got some creature between his front paws.

Sunday was a good example. Because I was ready for church early, I was reading. Chesterfield had been begging me to let him in, but I ignored his yowls. It' a game we play. He insists he's there and I pretend he isn't. I've gotten quite good at it and nearly always win. Suddenly I heard an awful crash against the side of the house where the furnace chimney and a bed of hostas are. Chesterfield had gone from the kitchen door and the deck to the ground, and hit the house running in order to capture a young squirrel. Split-second timing. No blood spilled. A clean kill. Chesterfield leaves no marks on his prey.

Of course, being a cat he brought the dead squirrel to the door for my praise, but that's Allen's job. Since Allen was out of town, Chesterfield got little more than a nod from me. When I left for church, he had begun eating the squirrel. He almost always eats what he kills; he is no recreational hunter. Occasionally Chesterfield doesn't wait for the animal to die before tearing into it. Occasionally he doesn't wait for death to present his catch, either. Recently he dropped a live mouse at Greg's feet, which promptly ran off. Greg hooted and laughed and hissed at Chesterfield. What a stupid thing for a smart cat to do. Chesterfield half-heartedly tried to re-cover his poise and his prey, but he never wastes time nursing his injured pride. He quietly began to wash himself, as if to say, "Maybe next time; I'd better get my coat ready." Even for cats, pride can sometimes go before a fall.

I don't like death in the sunshine when the scent of newly opened peonies is on the breeze. The stench doesn't fit. I didn't like it on Sunday. I don't like it after Easter. I don't like it when the longing for the garden is so strong. Death should be hidden away, like animals who grow old and die where no one can see them. Death, however, is still a public matter.

9 June Sightings

We don't pay enough attention to color. As June enters every year, I realize how hungry I am for color, the more intense the better—the deep orange and citron of my American lilies, the raspberry of my peonies. Most of us see the world in the basics: green, brown, blue, yellow. A tree is green, the earth is brown, the sky is blue, the sun is yellow; yet, we're nearly color-blind.

God, however, is more color-sensitive. As we were eating dinner outside recently, I noticed how different he made the green of a maple tree from that of a black walnut. How dull the world would be with but a few colors. Nature shows a myriad of greens, browns, and blues, as well as reds and yellows. If an interior decorator put maple green and black walnut green next to each other, we might complain that they clash, but somehow the colors work when God blends them. We have days in Michigan when the sky, so deep and clear, hurts the eye. At other times the sky is the same faded denim found in more southern climates. The color of the earth varies greatly, too, from the blackness of the celery fields to the nearly white sand of the beach.

I love working with color and studying how master painters such as Monet use it. Perhaps this is why I love the French Impressionists best. They tried to isolate color and object. If I painted, my canvases would reflect geometry in the most vocal colors I could mix. Since I can't, I practice the ancient arts of needlepoint and crochet; the colors I choose are always more important to me than the patterns. Textile manufacturers dye fabrics or yarns by blending several different colors to achieve the ones they want. Persian wool, the yarn used for needlepoint, for example, comes in several shades of green, some distinctly red, others blueish, and still others yellowlike. Browns may veer toward red or green. When working with color, the invisible shades mean as much as the visible ones.

But we can't see color at night. Actually we don't see color at all. According to scientists, color results in the mind from a complex exchange between light and object, eye and brain. Without light waves—the electromagnetic spectrum bouncing against, refracted, absorbed, or reflected by objects—we would lack color. Each object contains pigment that has a different molecular structure which reacts to light, producing heat, producing, ultimately, what we call color. As with so much else, we owe to Isaac Newton the foundation of our understanding about light, color, and optics. Although an eye doesn't actually see color, any more than it actually sees anything, in its retina exist rods and cones. Rods turn light into black and white; we need cones to send color messages to the brain. Cones are weak in dim light. Thus, color comes with the dawn. Color comes with light. At night, even under strong artificial light, color changes, becomes dull, and disappears: red turns to rust, deep purple to brown. Artists insist that natural light is necessary for any color work. Perhaps because I want color around me—any tint, any hue—I prefer days to evenings. As Goethe wrote, "Everything in life strives for color"—whether people or plants. Colors may clash and fight, or they may surrender, agreeing to peaceful coexistence: magentas, oranges, blues, purples, yellows, peaches, greens. They shout, Look at me! I'm more vivid than you. Or, I'm more restful or Have you ever seen such joy? What wonderful words they speak, words from God.

Since the ancient Chinese or the Greeks, we have believed that colors are symbols. Psychologists now study the influence of color on people. Some even speculate that each of us has a particular, though invisible, color surrounding him or her. We could literally reveal our true colors, but what kind of light would it take for us to see them? Remember: no light, no color. Would it take a light as strong as our sun? Or stronger? How about the Light of the World? No other will do. Crimson becomes snow-like. Drab browns or dirty yellows sparkle. The Light of the World turns night into day and lets the colors shine.

God creates all colors with his clean light; without them the world would be ugly. I thank God for this gift by noticing his colors, by acknowledging blue or purple people, green or mauve people, hot pink or pastel yellow people. Even beige and taupe people deserve recognition. What are the true colors of the people who surround you?

When people plan a flower bed, so horticulturalists tell us, they should think about color. Unfortunately, we can't plan our families or our offices in the same way, yet why ask orange and red to live comfortably side by side without expecting a few clashes along the way? Add some white or blue, maybe even a little yellow, and orange and red blend beautifully. Would human relationships be easier if we thought of each other as abstract colors or slightly stubborn, awkward plants whose genetics have created some color aberrations? We couldn't be any farther behind than we are now.

Because people aren't plants, we can't as readily see the colors of human beings as we can a chrysanthemum's. If we don't want a mum to bloom too early, we simply pick off the buds. How can we determine when a person will flower? Or what color he will be? When plants start behaving like people, though—unpredictable, irrascible—gardeners begin to mutter.

Some gardeners don't have intractable plants; my father's plants don't dare disobey him. Wherever he has lived, with whatever soil, his gardens have always succeeded. He could grow tomatoes out of rock. I recall only one time he had any trouble and only with America's favorite vegetable. When his tomatoes failed two years in a row, he had the county agent test the soil, then made some adjustments, and had no problems thereafter. His lawn was always greener, his corn always higher, his cabbages always heavier than anyone else's.

My sister has inherited the trait. She sticks a plant in the ground and it grows—name any kind: roses (without spraying, picking off bugs, whatever), forsythia, cucumbers, lettuce and spinach, any and all houseplants. I've always wished for a little of this. Plants grow for me, but only if I cater to them. Stephanie rarely weeds or uses much fertilizer. Her tomatoes grow beautifully in pot or shade. If I leave my borders alone for a week, the weeds overrun the plants.

I'm especially puzzled by three coneflowers in my front flower bed. Coneflowers, related to the black-eyed Susan with leaves of similar texture and flowers of a similar shape, are a cinch to grow. Pink with black eyes, coneflowers should be about three feet tall and bushy. At least that's what the horticulture books say. Only one of mine fits the description. I planted all three within two feet of each other, too close, I know, but I was in a hurry to fill the space. Yet that short distance makes a world of difference. The coneflower on the left is large, bushy, and luxuriant. The one to the right is less than a third its size. Each spring when the plants put up new shoots I watch to see if the runt is gaining ground, but always when the one plant is a foot-and-a-half tall, the other is struggling to reach six inches.

Three plants in the same soil in the same location; each receive approximately the same amount of sun and water; yet each is so different. I wish Jesus had told a parable about that. I understand why seed planted in different soil would produce different results. But why in the same soil? (Parents, too, might like to know.) When I started gardening in earnest a few years ago, it never occurred to me that plants wouldn't do what they were bred to do: people yes, plants no. Surely plants' characteristics are trapped in seed, only waiting germination to show who and what they are. A robin is never born blue; migrating birds follow their built-in instincts. Yet many of my plantings have not lived up to their billing.

Several springs ago, among some brambles beneath the heavy branches of black walnuts, I found dozens of bearded iris—blooming. Although they demand sunlight, these old-fashioned iris, obviously planted forty or more years ago before hybridizing took over the trade, were blooming beautifully. Since Allen and I planned to put a rhododendron bed in that particular spot, my mother-in-law dug them up and moved them to their ideal location: gritty soil and lots of sun. They haven't bloomed since. Maybe next June. Gardening brings me more questions than it does answers about the way God works. He is as inexplicable and unpredictable as my iris—no, more so.

Apparently, a little difference can make a big one. According to science writer K. C. Cole, one electron in the outer shell of an atom is the difference between sodium, a chemically active gas, and neon, one that is inactive. Change the wavelength of light just slightly and blue becomes violet.

Slight physical variations significantly alter nature, or at least the way we understand it. Recent experiments show that the sun may not be exactly round; if so, Einstein's view of the universe is dead. A slight variation in sound vibration determines whether a singer or instrumentalist is sharp, flat, or on pitch. A slight miscalculation when driving a car can have deadly results. It's the same with the tongue. Slight variations in its shape can also have deadly results. When I was learning to sing, the most difficult skill I practiced—I never mastered it completely—was how to control my tongue. Where and how the tongue lies in the mouth greatly affects the sound of the human voice. Even small adjustments make a big difference. For example, a misplaced tongue significantly reduces the space inside the head where the sound vibrates and echoes. Classical singers, who can't rely on a microphone or an echo chamber, have what God gave them and nothing else to project the sound. Attend a concert of a great singer, and you will hear what I mean. But let the tongue get in the way and the sound is strangulated—small, tight. The rich buoyancy of a beautiful voice disappears. A few lessons on how to use the tongue while singing will convince anyone how uncontrollable the tongue is. Few of us ever master that muscle.

Each word we say requires a different shape of the tongue. Some of us naturally curve our tongues around pleasant, helpful syllables; others of us find it difficult to put our tongues in a positive position. The difference between help and hurt may be the smallest difference between the sound of love or the shape of hate. Which syllable have we said? We may not know until we see the results.

One of the healthful things about gardening, over and above the food or flowers produced, is the practice it gives the tongue to form life-giving, love-sharing syllables. As with a farmer, a gardener knows that his success or failure lies with God. He provides moisture, warmth, nutrients, bacteria, and light. Expressing gratitude for good crops is the best tongue-strengthening exercise I know. But what about the failures? That's when we practice another tongue-builder—curbing the tongue so that we don't complain about all the things God failed to send our garden.

The tongue receives lots of exercise, too, in answering the common questions other gardeners ask. How does your garden grow? How's the corn coming? Have any tomatoes yet? Because we measure our success or failure by how our fellows fare, we gardeners need to know. Often gardening becomes a game of "I did it first," though all in fun, all in delight. At the beginning of the season, gardeners race to see who can plant the earliest, always a gamble against nature as well as our competitors. Can we beat the frost odds yet again? And then those wonderful new toys for gardeners—grow tunnels, hot caps, Remay—make it possible to plant earlier and earlier and then extend the season later and later, and thus enjoy mammoth, mouth-watering, tangy tomatoes before and after your neighbor has a blossom. At our place we play the game tolerably well, using only a few toys and tricks to help us along. Although each year we bemoan our slow start—our garden lies on low ground and dries slowly in the spring—we usually end up with a large harvest.

A vegetable garden is a fine thing in full bloom. Some people think it more beautiful than the most glorious lilies or the cheeriest geraniums. Best of all, it's edible. God ordered us out of his garden to earn our food by the toil of our bodies. Gardening may be hard work, but it's beautiful, satisfying work, too, this attempt to re-create what we lost when we sinned. I wouldn't go so far as to claim that my dying potato vines can match my tall phlox or black dragon lilies for beauty, but there is something aesthetically pleasing about neat rows of tas-seling corn or flowering pole beans. In theory, a vege-table garden saves money. No longer must a gardener cart home loads of tasteless head lettuce or canned beets, limp yellow beans or corn that has long since turned to starch. He need never take a chance that the melon he thumped and smelled is unripe. A perfectly ripened, homegrown melon slips quietly off the vine and rests, waiting for the table.

Even the best plans and newest garden aids, though, won't help a garden grow without a basic ingredient—rain. For four years we've had drought. It's hard to save money with a garden when even our low-lying plot needs daily watering. Because we have a well, we don't pay for the water directly; nor do we worry about bans on watering. But we've got to pump the water out of the well, and electricity doesn't come cheap in our area. However, our gardening mania doesn't begin or end with vegetables. Hydrangeas, hollies, rhododendron, hostas, azaleas, mock orange, veronica, dianthis, achil-lea, clematis, grass, crab apple trees, wisteria, lilacs, iris, peonies—to name a few (I did use the word mania)—need water, some every day. Plants may thrive in sun or shade, with or without fertilizer, but they can't do without rain. Remember that exercise on curbing the tongue? There's nothing like living with plants—and the people who grow them—to give a person lots of practice.

An up-to-the-minute bulletin. When I first wrote this, we were indeed suffering from a bad drought. Yet, drought or not, we had a splendid garden, the best we'd ever produced. Then came the summer of 1986, for us a wash-out—literally. Early in the spring it rained nearly every day, for about a month and a half. Our low-lying garden was constantly flooded. My early plants struggled to survive, as did a new flower bed facing the garden. Allen and I couldn't plant tomatoes until June, and then, a few days after we put fifty-three plants in the ground, it rained some more—two feet of water stood on the garden for days. I lost all but three plants. We replaced the others. It flooded again. We replanted beans and corn. It rained some more. To date, we have harvested enough lettuce for a few salads along with a handful of yellow beans planted as an experiment in the sandy bed next to the melons and winter squash. The melon plants have grown little, despite the rain; we lacked enough sun and warmth. Of the twenty-four new asparagus plants Allen spent a day planting, one survived. This year we will not harvest any corn, beans, pattypan squash, beets, carrots, peas, or tomatoes. Our garden is overrun with weeds, and we plan to till it under, planting field rye grass as a green manure crop; we hope for better things next year. (And we thought drought a tongue-curbing exercise.)

We have learned something about rain. For all our bitter complaints about four years of drought, we managed, we watered, we walked in the garden. In 1986 the garden never dried out; parts of it remained soggy until October.

Rain—either too little or too much—is the main problem with gardening. Although we can add water, we can't take it away. A few dollars spent watering the corn or the tomatoes pays for itself eventually. Rain is rather like confession of sin, something we agree is good for us, but something we'd rather let someone else do. On the other hand, a self-absorbed person, so introspective, so analytical about his guilts, weaknesses, and faults, so breast-beating and brow-wiping, drowns any benefit confession might have had. He saturates his soul with too many tears. Never again will we complain about too little rain. We've got to get this dying and confessing business right in one month or other, if not during Advent or Lent, then now. Nevertheless, perverse creatures that we are, we long for something to complain about. If we receive the right amount of rain, and all fifty tomato plants survive, we can always complain about too many tomatoes.

W hen I was growing up, my mother kept herself well-stocked with some too-manies—too many tomatoes, too many beans, too many pumpkins, too many peas, too many ears of corn. When it comes to gardens, my father doesn't understand the words *small*, *self-contained*, or *just enough*. I recall mother spending most of her summer over a hot stove, canning tomatoes, freezing beans, making pickles. No one can make pickles like my mother. As Greg said after he tasted some, "I'm never going to eat store-bought again." (He eats a jar of her sweet pickles at a sitting.) Looking back, I don't know why she didn't make us help her can, though knowing how we would have squawked I can understand why she thought it easier to work alone. I'm sure it was hard enough to get us to pick and snip beans or shell peas. In those years I thought leaf lettuce a poor substitute for iceberg and wouldn't touch a tomato even if it were the only food in the house.

I recall one advantage to her solitary canning: my sisters and I were stuck with brother duty—I, as the oldest, most often. Watching Steven was not easy. He was independent from his first determined breath on earth. Although some of us try to disguise our independence, he gloried in it—a glory that reached its apex in the summer, with warm weather and plenty of play-mates. No child has ever been more ingenious about the mischief he committed. Eventually he and I came to an unspoken understanding. My grandmother, who is what people used to call strong-minded, didn't know about it, though. Nor would she have approved any compromises between a four-year-old and a sixteen-year-old. On one of her all-too-infrequent summer visits, Grandma's strong-mindedness, my brother's independence, and our little agreement clashed.

Steven followed a strict summer routine from which he never deviated. After breakfast he went outside to play, which meant more to him, spatially, than it meant to Grandma. She carried her conservative theology into every area of her life: outside meant our yard and nowhere else. Steven, with a more liberal theological perspective, viewed such notions of space as parochial. Outside was anywhere he ventured—a neighbor's down the street or down several streets, the school playground, the baseball diamond. He freewheeled his way around our small town with the panache of a poker player.

As I said, Steven never varied his schedule. He left after breakfast and by 11:30, when he was hungry, he returned. He didn't need a digital watch that beeped and buzzed to let him know when it was time to do what; he lived the natural way of most little boys—by his stomach. Breakfast only lasted so long before he needed his noontime pick-me-up of *Winnie the Pooh* and a peanut butter and liverwurst sandwich with plain soup (by which he meant Campbell's tomato made with milk).

I accepted this because I didn't want him underfoot while I tried to finish my morning chores—dishes, cleaning, ironing, picking beans. My mother had a rule that if we finished our chores in the morning, we could do what we wanted in the afternoon, and what I wanted was to be at the pool no later than 1:00 P.M., book in hand. When Steven undid everything I did, I never made it.

But Grandma couldn't accept any of this. To her, Steven was a small child wandering around outside unsupervised. Why was she so nervous? We didn't live in a village any larger than the one she came from. About 11:00 she'd start to fidget. "Where is Steven?" she'd ask me. "I'll call him," I said. So I stood on the porch and called, unsurprised that he never answered. I explained that Steven would be home soon. Grandma wasn't satisfied. "Go look for him," she suggested. I didn't see the need.

Adults and kids often see needs differently. When I failed to persuade her, I agreed to go find him. But before I got off the porch, Steven was back, right on schedule. "Isn't lunch ready?" he asked. Grandma was not put off. She told Steven how worried we'd been (we?) because he was lost. Steven looked at her gravely and replied, "No I wasn't Grandma. I knew where I was all the time."

Lost is something little children understand well. They know when they are, and they know when they aren't. As we grow older, we forget the distinctions between the two. All the world is a muddy gray; gone are the clear colors of youth, the clear syllables our tongues formed. Grandmas always want to tell us we're lost; at times we may even agree. Often, though, we appear lost to those around us when we know exactly where we are and why we're headed in a particular direction. We're flower beds in the process of growing. We're colors just coming to light. We're creatures of God learning what he has to teach us, even when we don't want to learn, or find the lessons difficult to understand. We may at times be uncertain of where we are and whether we're lost. But God knows, and he is gracious enough to give us the space and the time to find our way.

10 July Offerings

I t took a long time for people to believe that there was such a thing as a microworld. Those who originally proposed the idea were ridiculed. Blame a disease on something we couldn't see? No one could imagine it. Now, of course, even the smallest child knows about bacteria and viruses.

Bacteria is an ugly word. We've learned to fear them, to fight them, to dose ourselves against them, and to douse our soil to kill them. Maybe we're anxious to arm ourselves against their effect because we can't see bacteria. Even when we don't need antibiotics, we take them—just in case. Doctors prescribe them for colds or influenza, even though such diseases are viral, not bacterial, infections. Then, when we really need antibiotics, our bodies have built up resistance; we've disarmed antibiotics.

Although harmful bacteria exist everywhere, we breathe quantities daily with few ill effects. But we've reasoned that if bacteria can harm us, it can also harm our soil. So we want to clean it up. Let's not have any dirty dirt, thank you. A dose of a good chemical is just what we need: no more organisms or bacteria rampant in our soil. True, certain diseases are carried through the soil, but how many bacteria actually do injury? Not many. Most of the earth's bacteria are necessary. Soil scientists speculate that the odds are 10,000 to 1 for benefiting from bacteria, not from being harmed by them. The soil needs bacteria for fertility; why kill the beneficent bacteria just to remove a few pesky ones?

Doctors are discovering the same principle. More and more people are living nightmare-like lives because of chemical overuse. Any exposure to man-made chemicals or to life outside a sterile environment means almost certain death to these people: They have developed a deadly allergy to life. Scientists studying the phenomenon have discovered that each person's problem began with an ordinary prescription for an antibiotic. Commonplace stuff. Yet the antibiotic altered his body's ability to handle bad bacteria and reduced the effectiveness of beneficial bacteria. No one knows yet how to reverse the process.

Yes, bacteria can be harmful, but not always. Our bodies, as well as our soil, need them. Maybe it's time to leave the bacteria alone. I wonder about this each July when our peppers are getting fruits and our early corn is ripening. Should I spray? Should I disinfect?

What we've done with our bodies and our soil we've done with our souls. We've declared bacteria bad, whether it comes as unseen airborne microbes, suffering, or physical stress. Walking puts stress on the heart, breathing demands labor from our lungs. Those who try to avoid difficult physical effort end up with a weak heart and flabby muscles, unlike those who accept the physical stress of living. So with suffering. None of us willingly undergoes suffering—quite the reverse. We believe that we have an inalienable right to live in a trouble-free environment, no matter how sterile it might eventually become.

But what about the stress we bring on ourselves through sin, selfishness, and insincerity? How do we rid ourselves of those problems? The only way I know is confession. But contemplating our weaknesses produces more stress, so most people suffer the curse rather than take the cure. No one wants to hear a negative message; certainly no one wants to impose such a spiritual discipline on himself, not in these days of antibiotics. It may be more difficult, but healthier ultimately, to deal one at a time with bad bacterium than to douse the Christian life with a universal disinfectant.

B ecause it uses waste, I like the idea of compost. Garbage becomes the soil of life when allowed to decompose. Allen plows it back into the ground, and we reap the benefits the following year in heartier corn and rounder, sweeter melons. Then the waste from that produce becomes, in turn, more compost for more food. Even before we had emptied our compost into the garden this year, it began producing. Somehow, whether through a bad potato we threw into the bin or a dead potato vine that wasn't quite as dead as we thought, we have potatoes growing in the compost bin, potatoes bigger than those in the garden. We placed our compost bin at the back of the garden under a tree where it almost blends into the woods. Along with the potatoes, covering and beautifying the bin, we have the most luxuriant flowering squash vine. Will it bear fruit? Maybe not, but it turns an eyesore into a sight for sore eyes. This is what happens when God takes over.

Compost has wonderful properties. Yes, it smells unpleasant—at first. Yes, it looks ugly and unattractive—at first. Yet as it decomposes it changes, transformed into the stuff of life. There is no richer, more fertile material to put in the garden than compost. The organisms in compost, the bacteria, the stuff we're always trying to kill, join the organisms of ordinary garden soil to fertilize and enhance it. The earth is alive with potential for growth, increased when regularly fed with compost. The dark crumbly matter no longer smells unhealthy but has a good, clean earth scent. Because it looks and feels so unlike what it was to begin with—leftover lettuce, watermelon rinds, grass clippings—we hardly believe this can be the same stuff.

Waste products may not smell good; compost decomposing may not be the most beautiful sight. Yet, if we could as easily see and smell our sins as we can compost, we might not only avoid a few more sins than we do, we might also become less discouraged at those we don't. God has a marvelous way of taking all those smelly sins and decomposing them for our good. He plows our composted sins back into our lives for our renewed growth and vitality. But it takes as long as the compost in our back garden. God wants to build up our soil permanently. There's no better way to grow the sweetest fruit or the most beautiful vines than the compost God lavishes on us. He takes our impatience and anger, reduces it to rubble, and gives it back to us as stamina to bear sorrow, or energy to create life. I attack weeds with ferocity and determination when God helps me use anger positively. My bread never rises so high as when I take out all my frustration on it rather than on my family.

That's the business of God, the compost business. No one does it better than he. But then, we supply him so much usable material. In just a day we waste so much of ourselves—at least I do. I waste daylight by hiding myself indoors. I waste time fretting over my inadequacies. I waste my mind worrying needlessly about the future. I waste friendships when I fail to write or call. I waste my intelligence by refusing to think or by reading ignorant books. I waste my soul in hatred or jealousy. I waste my spirit when I refuse to laugh. In a year, the waste is mountainous.

I'm a failure at kindness, gentleness, and patience, particularly in my own family where they have to put up with me. Isn't that true in all families? Most of us have company manners and family manners, as we have company menus and family menus. Just look at James and his family.

James thought about all the bad manners he had seen this morning. He slowed to a walk, noticing that he was in what seemed to be a park, one he'd never seen before. When he'd run out of the house, trying to force the tears back inside his eyes where his older brother told him they belonged, he had paid little attention to where he was going. He had planned to head for his little fishing hole and crawl into the arms of old mother willow. But by the time he'd slowed down and looked around him, by now having successfully trapped his tears somewhere deep in his eye sockets, he had no idea where he was.

Probably lost, he thought. *And it's all their fault.* It always was. Yet, despite his drowning eyes, James liked what he saw. The trees looked friendly, waving their limbs at him as he walked by. He didn't see any willows, but the jaunty birch, maple, and beech trees cheered him more than old mother willow might have, though she *was* such a comfort. Nothing there interrupted James while he catalogued how mean people were to him.

Perky periwinkles and saucy black-eyed Susans winked and swayed as he brushed past their leaves. He knew what they were because Mother grew them. He remembered how she liked their colors. This park de-manded joy and sucked sadness out of a person's soul.

Despite his best intentions, James was beginning to forget why he had rushed out of his house so quickly, which was peculiar because James treasured his hurts. He remembered what people had said or done to him for a long, long time—but only the bad things. He never remembered the good things; in fact, he believed only bad things ever happened to him. He was quite ordinary in that respect.

If the truth must be said, James loved to be hurt. Of course, he didn't know this—he was still too young—but his mother wasn't. She reinforced his bad habit by telling his father and sisters and brothers that he was sensitive and artistic. His siblings thought he was a baby pain in the neck, while his father knew James wanted attention. His father knew James manipulated people, particularly his mother. His father just knew. And that's what bothered James. When he looked at his father's eyes, James found it hard to love his hurts quite so much as before.

But away from his father's eyes, he could travel his comfortable road. So he did. *No one understands me*, he muttered to himself. *Everybody picks on me. I can't help it if I'm absentminded. I don't mean to break things. Jon thinks I broke his stupid old record on purpose. I wish I had now. I don't know why he won't let me come into his room.* James punctuated his thoughts with an occasional gulp and a sigh. Then as thoughts of his father crossed his path again, James stumbled a little in his flight.

Up ahead, past the cheery wildflowers and bowing trees, James saw a small bridge. He loved bridges, why he didn't know. He broke into a trot again. As he reached the middle of the bridge, he looked down hoping to see a fish or a snapping turtle, maybe a frog. *Wouldn't Marsha hate to find a frog in her bed. That would fix her. Marsha is worse than Jon, the way she treats me.*

Sure enough there was a big, ugly, slimy, snapping turtle. *Perfect.* James had never seen a more perfect re-

venge just sitting there staring at him. He wasn't afraid
of snapping things, or slimy things either. He'd always
been able to take his fish off the hook, because his father
had taught him how their first fishing trip. But just as
James went to grab the turtle, something else caught his
attention. He shook his head and blinked his eyes several
times, but that didn't help. He couldn't be seeing what
he was seeing; but no matter how hard he blinked his
eyes, the face wouldn't go away. *If anybody's face should
be in the water*, he thought, *it should be mine.* But instead
of his own long nose and shaggy hair, his father's round
eyes and cleft chin stared at him and would not let him
go.

With a halfhearted sigh, James stood up to leave without the turtle.

The turtle, who had been certain that his end was in
sight, breathed a much bigger sigh and slowly swam
under the strange log that had so mysteriously appeared
in the water.

James had a lot of ingredients for good compost, if
he'd only known. Maybe when he's older, and if he keeps
looking at his father's eyes, he'll know it. And be glad
for the composting.

Most of us could give a daily tally of the scraps left
over from our meals. Some cantaloupe rind, a few
banana peels, those last few mouthfuls of rice no one
wanted. What about the potato peelings, the asparagus
stalks, or the carrot scrapings? How many eggs did we
have for breakfast or use in making oatmeal muffins for
supper? A lot of waste going to waste. But what about
the non-food scraps we've been ignoring over there in
the corner of our soul, or the nasty thoughts we tossed
into the back room of our mind? When we add up that
stuff over a year, we find a lot of compost to put in God's
hands.

A day is bad enough. A few months or a year can be

even worse. No matter what the season, I seem to have some leftovers in my life. I don't like them, either in myself or in my refrigerator. Maybe that's the real reason we started a compost bin—to rid ourselves of unsightly leftovers and yet not waste them. We almost delight in what we have to toss into the wire bin behind the garden. And our trash bags are not as full or in as much danger of bursting open as they once were. We are learning to value what seems valueless. Now if we could only learn to relinquish the ingredients God needs to cook up his compost. Eventually the stuff might even help me grow some patience.

I needed more patience than I had when we decided to clip Greg's tonsils (that's his verb). "Human nature is perverse," I told him. Although we love ourselves better than we love anyone or anything else, we continually behave toward ourselves in harmful ways. It's a strange kind of love—not the kind of love God has for us, or the kind of love a parent has for a child. That sort challenges, demands, comforts, sacrifices, encourages: whom God loves he disciplines. The love we have for ourselves lives on easy street up the soft path of good intentions. It's the opposite of the compost principle. We don't demand enough of ourselves: If something is difficult, avoid it; if something is simple, embrace it.

So I've told Greg. And told Greg. He wants to do what he wants to do. He wants to live on easy street—no homework, lots of baseball, and *Sports Illustrated* un-limited—and make his own rules, which is to say he doesn't want any rules, certainly no responsibility. (His brother, Allen, is the same way—and so am I, I must admit.)

Because Greg lacks some inner toughness to do what's best for himself, he's had a difficult time. After years of suffering with strep infections and many, many days of missed school, we had his tonsils removed. But contrary to the orders of doctors, nurses, and us, he refused to eat or drink. Because Greg thought it was stupid to swallow when it hurt, he didn't. As a result, his throat muscles began to heal tight as a fist, which only made the pain worse when he could no longer avoid food or drink. Although it was easier not to swallow, it was short-term ease and long-term hurt.

Jesus told us to love our neighbors as ourselves. We believe we can't obey because we don't love ourselves enough. But perhaps Jesus meant that we were to love our neighbors sacrificially as we should love ourselves sacrificially. Each hard task we accomplish ensures new strength and endurance for our muscles. Greg's throat would have been better off had he practiced this principle. Why do we never expect difficulties to become fertilizer for fruitful living?

We see this composting principle throughout creation. The Kirtland's warbler, which lives in the pine barrens of north-central Michigan, depends on forest fires to provide its nesting sights. A species of pine in northern California only releases its pine cones to reseed itself after a forest fire has killed the original trees. That sounds very much like nature's version of losing your life to find it; that sounds like good bacteria, fruitful waste products, and the rich potential of trash. Somehow, though, we never expect it to work, no matter how often or in how many ways God tells us it will. Maybe if we did, more of us would swallow, even when it hurts.

11 August Refreshment

M y birthday is in August. So is my mother's. Several of my cousins were born in August. In years past we've held an August birthday picnic for our extended family. Some of the now out-of-town cousins have occasionally returned for the feast.

We always fuss for a birthday. No one should have to work on his birthday. At our house, the birthday person eats his favorite foods and is feted: the one day in the year for total self-centeredness. Didn't the world come to a halt—the particular world into which we were born—twenty, thirty, or more years ago?

This year when we arrived at my mother's house for her birthday dinner, she announced, "We're having chicken because that's my favorite and it's my birthday." Now there's the right attitude. Greg, who has been learning to cook and bake, wanted to make Grandma a pie for her birthday. He made two, blueberry and nectarine, his surprise present for her. The pies were delicious, the crust better than most adults can make. My mother, one of the best pie bakers ever, was impressed.

So when August arrives, I think a lot about my growing up. When a person is growing up, no one can predict what he'll carry with him from his upbringing. Will Greg grow up to bake pies? Will he do most of the cooking in his house the way my brother does in his? Or will he become traditional and let his wife do it all?

We waste time in school, believing we'll never use all that information about Khatmandu or the Sudan interior. Then along comes Trivial Pursuit or a book about narwhals and as adults we're fascinated. If only we could anticipate what we'll need and want to know, life would be much easier. I certainly feel that way. Fortunately, I started to cook when I was twelve, but in other areas I've had some handicaps to overcome: not enough history, science, or math—subjects I now read on my own.

Every child has a favorite hated chore. Mine was picking produce from the garden; I think that's right up there on our kids' list of favorite hates. I went to great lengths to avoid it—volunteered to scrub the kitchen floor, clean the bathrooms, almost anything, just so long as I didn't have to get out in the hot, humid Pennsylvania weather amid the bugs and furry green leaves of bean plants and cucumber vines. It only took an afternoon among the beans for me to itch for days afterward. The stooping and the bending and the bugs and the itching drove me to swear that I would never have a garden.

I stuck to my word as long as I could. Naturally, when I lived in Manhattan or in a townhouse, I wasn't tempted much. But as soon as we had enough land we started a garden, which has grown bigger each year and then begun to reproduce so that now we have three vegetable gardens, plus numerous flowerbeds. So much for famous last words, as I tried to tell Allen Jr.

There was no convincing him that he might indeed grow up to have a garden, or—what might even be worse so far as he is concerned—a compost heap. "Look what happened to me," I said. He remained unimpressed. Yet, not only do I have a garden—or gardens—I enjoy them. I even like picking produce. Of course, I grow more pole beans than bush beans. "Why," I asked my mother, "did I spend so many years bending over bush beans when God also made pole beans?" "We don't like them as well," she said. To have an alternative to stooping, I would have adjusted my taste buds.

When we're young, we don't see alternatives—or at least not the same alternatives our parents see. Sometimes we insist on alternatives where there should be none, such as learning history or geography or geometry theorems. Although we have no alternative but to mature physically, we can choose to remain a child mentally and emotionally; or we can choose to become an adult and learn to like picking beans. Unfortunately, some of us choose without realizing it. We fall into the wrong alternative, whether from indolence or indifference, fear or irresponsibility. Only mature people can see alternatives, but even then only after the fact and not at the point of choice.

Picking beans is only one of many chores that we may dislike, though God may plan to have us pick a great many in our lives; he has lots of gardens. We may accept the task and acquiesce ungracefully, or refuse, only to change our minds at the last moment as did the workers in Jesus' parable. We can be thankful that even if we wait till the last minute to choose the correct alternative, God will still give us our full wages.

But parents are different. We don't have the luxury God does or the view. So when Greg or Allen refuse to do their chores or grumble or do them late, they don't receive their wages; they receive justice, not mercy. As a parent, I find it difficult to balance mercy and justice. We spend no little time explaining to Greg and Allen what mercy is and how God sends it daily. Then, when they complain that something isn't fair, we explain justice to them. I prefer mercy to justice. Do any of us really want fair treatment? Don't we really ask for special treatment, which is the result of mercy? But how do we teach a child responsibility, duty, love in action, moral behavior, and all those other virtues unless we use justice? Yet every time I do, something says to me, *Do you want God to treat you that way?* At times, in order to see more clearly, I need to step outside for a while.

E ach person at some point experiences a time when time stands still, when the sun doesn't move, when the breezes don't blow. Two hours or twenty—it doesn't matter. Time, just as much a creation of God as is space or sound or ourselves, takes a vacation.

I have always thought of time as fluid, as expanding or contracting. Twenty-four hours may be a rigid measurement, yet because each day is so varied some days seem to contain only twelve or fifteen hours, while other days last thirty-six hours or longer. This fluctuation of time makes life interesting; yet the times when time takes a breather are the most exhilarating times of all.

A sense of suspended time allows us to evaluate our circumstances, our goals, our values. For example, how should I behave as a parent? Hand in hand, we and time step aside from all those around us who continue to rush and rumble through their days unaware that time has shouted Stop! Ceasing to be of this world, we instead taste the tang of eternity: not a place of neverending time but a place of no time at all. God will transform our fellow creature, time, into what he was intended to be in Eden, just as he will transform us. Sometimes, though, we miss time's shout. Teetering on the edge of time scares us; how can we breathe in a place that smacks too much of a vacuum? So we rush to fill the corners and patch the cracks with unnecessary and distracting bric-a-brac—most of it cheap, tawdry, ugly.

Now is the time for silence and prayer, the chance to follow Paul's suggestion in Philippians—to think on the beautiful, the pure, the lovely, and to rid ourselves of the clutter. Attuning ourselves to time and awaiting its word to stop can be the best use of our time. But what if time tells us to stop while the rest of our lives shout Go? The most natural time to stop time is on vacation, if we can wait that long. But how many of us rest on vacation? Some people travel, wearing themselves out sightseeing. Others choose a spot on the beach, though the spot comes with air conditioning, garbage disposal, night spots, and steep rent. Still others, spending most of their vacation driving, visit family. Often, vacation is not the respite we need.

I have a simple idea of vacation. First, it must be inexpensive. Second, it must be taken near water loaded with fish. Third, it must not be near any sights that need to be seen. Fourth, it shouldn't take more than a day's drive to reach. And then there's a fifth. I don't want a lot of people making demands of me. Sightseeing is work; driving is work; visiting is work. I don't want to do any work on vacation. I want to sit and read, sit and fish, sit and stare at the sun coming up over soft, silent water, sit and pray. I want to sit and be. Vacation is my chance to step outside with time and enter timelessness. Time and I wouldn't miss it for all the sights overseas.

Anne Morrow Lindbergh had the right idea when she isolated herself at the beach, her experiences recorded in the now classic book, *Gift from the Sea*. Walking gently so as not to disturb the world, we can learn—or relearn— how to listen to the silences in ourselves and in nature. We can study the thoughts of others by the books we choose. We can study the thoughts of God in the sashaying of leaves in the breeze or in the rhythm of rain on the roof: At least one rainy vacation day is always welcome. Simplicity makes such a vacation possible. Not for me beautifully appointed rooms or splendid meals. A sparsely furnished cottage, some bread and cheese, a little fruit; these are what I require on vacation, these and God's example, Jesus. He knew when to step away from the demands of his life. He walked the Galilean seashore or hid in the mountains. Most of us have neither the opportunity nor the discipline to separate ourselves as often as Jesus did, but for at least a week or two a year shouldn't we try?

Perhaps we fear empty spaces. We don't have room for spaces that serve no practical purpose—we don't want to make room. Empty spaces of all kinds make us uneasy. Whether a pause in a conversation, a few minutes or an hour or a week with nothing to do, a blank section of wall, or a bare spot in the soul—we want it filled. Winter is the unwelcome landscape of empty space. Because we see too easily through bare branches, leafless limbs, and vacant vines, many of us resent it—this spare season which haunts us with longing for sumptuous, profligate summer.

We equate emptiness with isolation, with loneliness, with lack. Something is missing, an empty stomach waiting for a rich meal. We don't understand an empty space that seems so much like nothingness or a vacuum where gravity doesn't exist. For many people, God is just another extraneous empty space; they don't see him, they don't hear him. Even when they've tried to talk to him, he never responds in language they understand. Maybe we have even felt this way. God is up there, somewhere, wherever that is, in a space as empty of activity as his voice is silent. Why would anyone want to join God in that great, silent, black hole which seems to be his home?

Yet without the empty spaces, the silent times, the spare landscape, we would never relax. As any musician will explain, the rests—the empty spaces in music—are more important than the notes. Sound is meaningless and rhythm nonexistent without the breaks in between. Life's empty spaces need not be meaningless or lonely or terrifying; they can be the rests that make sound beautiful and rhythm complex. In them God greets us most easily, provided we keep the empty spaces free.

Once we've conquered our fear of emptiness and learned to embrace silence, to rest comfortably in the stillness, we've got to come home. We may try to preserve our stillness, but after every trip, after every vacation, after every kind of absence, whether spiritual or physical, we must come home. Home always seems strange to me when I've been gone a while. I look forward to it and say with the rest of the world, "Boy, it's good to be home again." Yet part of me disagrees, vehemently denying its goodness. Everything I left behind is still here; everything I learned while I was away is evaporating in that messy closet I meant to clean before I left. It niggles at me. There are new weeds in the flower beds and the houseplants are half dead from lack of water. Although I left a clean house and a neat desk, in my absence they reverted to their natural, chaotic state. *How*? I wonder. Problems I refused to think about while away hit me full force as I head up the drive.

I always try to give myself a transition day, one more day of rest, but also a day to slowly return to normal. Sweep a floor, read a business periodical, bake some bread, think about work, schedules, routines, chores, cool weather, chopping wood, fires.

It doesn't matter so much how wonderful home is. Getting back is hard, harder for some than for others. Jesus had to go home early. By all accounts, heaven is a fair home to have, yet who of us would want to travel

Jesus' road home or start the trip as early as he did? He was scourged, humiliated, crucified; yet he had no other way to go home. Peter, too, had a tough time—his own fault, of course, like a lot of us. He left home when he denied Jesus three times. He lied, he rejected his Lord, he showed cowardice. Jesus had become his home, his place in life, his reason for being. For him, the road back was filled with tears and remorse, but also forgiveness.

Although not as hard as Peter's, my road back from vacation may also be hard. All roads leading back wind through rough terrain. Yet even when the trip is difficult, Jesus provides mercy along the way—no matter what the homecoming.

12   September Change

The faeries had done it again. As soon as she put her feet on the worn wood floors that morning, Ghia knew they had been in her room. She glanced at the calendar. September first. Every year without fail for the past five years the faeries had turned September into a changeling. August breezed along as Ghia expected August to do, then came September, which would misbehave.

Ghia stretched and shivered. She was glad now that something had told her to put on her snug white nightgown. If only she had shut the window a little last night, but the listening tree outside her window had said nothing of faeries or changelings or sharp air. Ghia shook her head at him, irritated that he had not warned her. He must have known something was up.

Dressing quickly in the warmest skirt and sweater she could find, Ghia stumbled into the kitchen where her mother had a fire going and porridge bubbling. Trifle, her ginger cat, yowled at Ghia's clumsy entrance. Her mother looked up.

"I see you found something warm to wear. Things certainly have changed since yesterday. Sit down and have some breakfast," she said.

"May I have brown sugar or maple syrup on my porridge? I know. The faeries have been here. I felt them on my floor."

"Ghia, how many times have I told you, no faery nonsense. The weather has just changed, that's all. And, yes, you may have syrup, but only a little. Now eat."

"It's still too hot. I think I'll let it cool," Ghia replied, as she gazed out the window. *What's happened to the leaves?* she wondered. Weather or no weather, leaves just don't change color overnight. But Ghia knew it was no use talking to her mother about what the faeries had done. She supposed her mother was too old to feel their presence. Ghia never wanted to be that old.

"That's all right," her mother said. "You've got plenty of time. Tom was over early to tell me the school burned down last night, and no one knows where or when you'll start back."

To most children her age, this would have been good news. But Ghia loved school; the faeries could have done nothing worse. What would she do? She had no books left to read and no money to buy more. The school library was gone now. Maybe she'd pretend to be the story girl and write her own; she'd been wanting to try anyway. Why must the faeries always choose September?

F or lots of us, September is a changeling month. Each year I long to return to the classroom in September. I always loved school, college better than high school, graduate school better than college. Ghia and I have that in common, though I don't believe in faeries and never had a listening tree outside my window. And I *don't* like maple syrup.

But I do like September and always have. September meant new routines, new courses, new people and teachers, new clothes, a new season. September was a month of change. Even today September is a larger month in our lives than most other months. Allen, a college professor, returns to school this month, Greg and Allen Jr. do, too. I've always been left behind, but not this year.

Two weeks ago, if anyone had asked me what this September would be like, I would have answered "the same old thing." Since I don't believe in faeries, I had no idea that September is a changeling; yet September knew something I didn't. Ask me today what September will be like and I'll answer "no idea." Or how about next September? Same reply, for now I know that September is a changeling. Two days ago I had no idea I would be teaching twenty-two college freshmen how to write clear sentences and paragraphs, how to write a research paper, or how to judge whether a piece of nonfiction is good or bad writing. But I am. I've begun reading a new textbook and rereading some of my favorite stylists. I've met my class, worked on the syllabus, and edited their first writing samples. What a changeling September is.

Most of us don't like change—at least not that drastic or that rapid. Give us a little control, a little warning, a little time to prepare. August has fooled us into thinking that summer stretches endlessly ahead. September sneaks up on us, taking unfair advantage. The tan hasn't started to fade when September dips into the forties and drops us, shivering, into the midst of change.

But just as forty-degree temperatures can invigorate us, so can change. We need some shaking up. We need someone to dump us out of the hammock, start our pulse jumping and our blood flowing faster than at August speeds. A change in weather, a change in attitude, a change in routine, a change in jobs can all do it. Yes, we want some warning, some time to prepare, but God doesn't always work that way. I'm certain that Peter wanted time to turn the budget over to someone else, but when Jesus said "follow me" he went, ready or not.

Although in a sense I'm unprepared to teach composition to college students, in another I've been preparing all my life. Writing and reading go together. If there is one thing I know how to do, it is read. When I was a child, my mother punished me by taking away my books and making me play outdoors because I enjoyed nothing more than a story. By the time I was ten or eleven, I was reading my mother's library of adult novels as well as every book my mother borrowed from the public library. I inherit my love of books from her; she used to climb an old tree to read where no one could find her. On a dairy farm there's always something to do; reading wasn't on my mother's list of chores. She even read while she washed dishes or while she practiced the piano; people who love to read will do anything for a sight of words.

I don't remember when I learned to read, though I do remember practicing how. Because Dick and Jane, our school texts, offered no challenge, I chose books with difficult words and read them repeatedly until I knew every one. Then I graduated myself to even harder books. Because mother was not one to answer a lot of questions, I learned early what dictionaries were for. The world of words was my favorite place, the place I longed to enter before I knew how, the place I never wanted to leave once I learned how to find it.

My sister Stephanie, on the other hand, remembers the exact time—almost to the minute and second—when she learned to read. Stephanie is two-and-a-half years younger than I; what I did, she had to do. So once I learned to read, she was determined not to be left behind. For example, she recalls her numerous—and unsuccessful—attempts to read road signs. Then, one day, she did: she looked at them; she read them; and she couldn't stop. Stephanie discovered that now she had no choice but to read. All road signs made sense to her, whether she wanted them to or not. She could never go back to the time when words meant nothing; she hadn't realized that was part of the bargain.

Stephanie was changed by learning to read a few simple road signs. It wasn't the last change she experienced. Words of all kinds change us; as the word *September* has changed me. Events and words are linked, whether going to college, moving, marrying, having children; none of us is ever the same afterward. Each experience begins with "I do," "I will," "I'll go"—words of intent, words of commitment, words that shouldn't be taken lightly. They're the sounds of change, hard sounds to master. Maybe I had the right idea when I was five; practicing hard words is the best way to ease ourselves into change.

O f all the changes September requires, though, changing places is the most difficult: home for college, college for career, my house to *our* house. When we're young, the idea of changing places is pleasant; when we're older, we find it uncomfortable. Many a child has grown up thinking that just about any place is more interesting than the place where he is. A neighbor's yard always looks better than his own. A house in the next block has more appeal. Relatives who live out-of-state, or people he knows through books, have exciting, adventurous lives. How can his brown-paper-bag-of-a-life ever compare? He's a child without change. The grass grows; his father makes him cut it. A page of algebra inexorably leads to the next. Word problems, noun declensions, diagramming sentences march on.

That's about all the sense of place any child has—a wistful longing to be someplace else. Once he grows up, he discovers that place is more important to a sense of self than time, which is why changing places is so difficult. Where do you come from? Where were you born? Answers to these questions explain much about a person. I'm from New England or the Midwest or Pennsylvania, I could answer truthfully, since I lived in all those places growing up. I was born in Virginia, however, so does that make me a Southerner? Not in any way I understand; I'm as Northern as they come. But even explaining that I'm from nowhere in particular says something about me: nomad, wanderer, a person longing for a place, someone tired of moving.

Coming from a particular place, say Lake Wobegon, Minnesota, or Suring, Wisconsin, or Galilee in Judea, explains how a person was raised, what attitudes his parents undoubtedly tried to instill in him, the scenery he looked at most of his life, the insects he swatted and sweated over in the summer, the fish he ate, the accent he spoke with. We can't escape our place; neither could Jesus or Peter. Can anything good come out of Nazareth? Jesus probably wished that he wasn't so marked by his place. Brilliant rabbis didn't come from Nazareth. People probably stopped listening when they heard his accent: wrong side of the country.

Peter's accent didn't help him, either. He was marked as a follower of Jesus the night Jesus was arrested, though Peter denied it. Yet it never does any good to pretend you're from some place else, no matter how much you dislike your home town. Jesus promised Peter and us a place that will satisfy everything we want. But how do they talk up there? Although we don't know, we could start to memorize the vocabulary, even if we can't get the accent quite right.

But that's for later, a place to long for and work toward.

In the meantime, we've got places to see and places to be that take more change than we're willing to undergo. Paul constantly talks to recalcitrant people about place. Take temples, for example. We're to be the temple of the Holy Spirit; now that's a tough place to be. Even though I grew up on sermons and Sunday school lessons about what that meant, it wasn't until a recent choir rehearsal that I began, faintly, to understand.

We were singing a simple setting of the hymn "Come Down O Love Divine." The text concludes: "We will never know God's grace until we *become the place* wherein the Holy Spirit dwells." Become the place. *What kind of place am I?* I wondered. What kinds of places do I know? I know my house, my office, my parent's house, my sister's house. I know Washington, D. C. and Chicago and Michigan—or at least parts of them. I know Manhattan—more than I'd like. I also go places—movies, restaurants, grocery stores, church. I know cold places and hot places, clean places and messy places, beautiful places and ugly places, places that change and places that stay the same. My house incorporates a lot of places into one place. A friend invites me to come over to her place. So much of my life is governed by a place or places, real and imagined.

But what kind of place am I? Am I the kind of place that makes it possible for me to know God's grace? Am I the kind of place another person would want to move into? Am I the kind of place the Holy Spirit would find roomy enough? Would I have spare, clean lines with sparkling windows and white, white walls? Or would I paper myself with ornate grass cloth and drape myself with brocade? Would the Holy Spirit prefer blue to pale green, early American to Scandinavian design? Am I drab and hollow-eyed, plaster cracking? Or am I well-patched, well-loved?

Probably the Holy Spirit has no preferences for color

or style or whether his place is old or young, so long as the furniture is honest, the carpet cared for, and the air filled with love. Then, once the Holy Spirit is settled in, the grace of God will care for the rest.

T he problem, of course, is how to keep the carpets vacuumed and the air from becoming stale with hate or the corners infested with cobwebs of lies. It's difficult enough in dealing with yourself, but when you're a parent you must also teach your children what kind of place to be. A sense of morality is difficult to convey to children. Given half a chance, a child will almost always choose the wrong course of action and then stand amazed when a parent insists he is wrong. Take the concept of truth and falsehood. What does it mean to tell the truth? If a parent asks a child, "Did you practice?" he could receive a yes, when the real truth might be, "I went through the motions but I didn't really pay attention or make any progress."

Stealing is usually an easier concept for children to understand. Or so I thought until the day Greg brought home a wooden bat from the park. When I asked him where he got it, he said some kid had left it at the ball field so he'd brought it home. "Otherwise," he added virtuously, "someone might steal it." "Right," I said, "you."

Greg couldn't understand why I said he had stolen the bat. The owner, after all, had carelessly forgotten it. But would Greg have returned to look for the bat had it been his? "Probably," was his reluctant answer. He just as reluctantly returned the bat to the place he found it. I doubt he ever really understood why he had to do so.

Too many of us live in the land of moral vagueness. We rationalize our behavior by calling it something else, just as Greg claimed he was saving the bat from theft by stealing it himself. Jesus understood how fond we are of this territory. He tried to get us to move by telling us, for example, that murder comes in many forms, physical or spiritual, and that unfaithfulness is a matter of the heart as well as the body. We're all literalists and Pharisees at bottom. We need a broader definition of morality not a narrower one. With a pharisaical view of righteousness, we can count ourselves pretty good guys. A broader definition forces us to stand with the tax collector—and we're uneasy with the company. The tax collector, though perhaps a business success, is a moral and social failure. The changeling, September, brings with it the potential for either one, success or failure: a new year, new classes, new job, new place, all unmarred by previous failures or colored by previous successes. Children face this in school. Parents face it, too, but from a different perspective: to help a child or let him flounder and possibly fail. How often do we explain right and wrong? How much do we let them find out by themselves? Did the tax collector's parents explain too much or too little?

Young children need a great deal of help, but when they reach junior and senior high age, parents hope that their children have become places where discipline and responsibility paper the walls. Although there will always be a project or two in which a parent must be involved—driving a teenager to a city library or helping build a science project—most teenagers should now be correcting their own spelling errors, faulty grammar, and punctuation. They shouldn't need constant supervision to complete assignments and chores.

Yet we fear failure so much, and fear it for our children, that we may overprotect them, trying to be their rooms even though failure may be the best lesson they can learn. A few summers ago Greg and Allen worked for a small fruit and vegetable farmer. They weeded and hoed, and picked beans, strawberries, and other fruits and vegetables. It was hot, dirty labor for children who had never worked hard in their lives. Yet they wanted to try. Allen Jr., though, was sloppy; his boss warned him that if his work didn't improve he would be fired. It didn't, and he was. That difficult lesson was one of the best. Allen began to clean the room where he lived. Each year the room has become more orderly, more disciplined, more responsible. I doubt that he would have begun to redecorate the place he is without such failure.

It was a hard lesson for us as parents, too, one we must relearn constantly. We want to do the redecorating, though sometimes the wall paper won't stick unless the child himself supplies the glue. I wonder if God occasionally faces this same problem with us.

Although September marks many annual changes for our family, the best one happens to Greg; he has a birthday. We close the month celebrating change, just as we open it anticipating change.

As I said, at our house we expect fanfare and presents on birthdays. Some years we celebrate so well that next year's celebration becomes a matter of what to do next. For Greg's twelfth birthday we and some friends chartered a boat and went fishing on Lake Michigan. He caught three of the six fish we brought home. Landing a salmon nearly as long as he was tall was a thrilling way for him to mark his birthday. That night we ate steak and salmon grilled over charcoal and talked about all those fish. Last year for his thirteenth birthday, we gave Greg waders and his first salmon fishing trip on the Pere Marquette River. This time he caught a forty-inch salmon on a ten-and-a-half foot fly rod rigged with a six-pound test line and an artificial lure. He took forty minutes to land the fish. Then, after it was tied to a nylon stringer while Greg was playing another salmon, his fish broke himself free—determined to die. Dismayed, Greg watched the salmon swim away to finish spawning. We consoled him with a birthday dinner of his choosing—cornish game hens in raspberry sauce, baked blue hubbard squash, and a three-layer pecan spice cake with pecan frosting—and Greg had a birthday celebration worthy of the name. This year it was another trip, a French beef stew, and the same kind of cake—a weekend celebration.

However, we can't mark every change in our lives with a party. Sometimes change occurs before we know it; or maybe we don't realize until long after that a big event has taken place. But as much as possible at our house we try to celebrate change, small or great. God has given us lots of precedent for doing so; no one knows how to throw a party as well as he. When was the last time you saw or heard choirs of angels? Or had three kings visit you? I've never received a box of gold on my birthday, have you? The birthday of mother earth sounds glorious—a week-long affair with each day bringing another marvelous change to the place we call home. "And it was good," said God. I guess it was. Even after that great change, the Fall, it's still not a bad place to be.

13   October Gifts

B aseball season is almost over. The leaves, having changed color, cover my drive and flower beds with God's mulch. Those last holdouts of summer, chrysanthemums, are finally fading. Now that days end sooner, seeing is more difficult. And yet there's still so much I want to see, so much I want to do before winter returns.

Allen and I have many regrets as we say good-bye to the last marvelous season of the year. The changes September started continue in October. We put away outdoor life and come inside. It's a month-long process, what with saying farewell to the balls and strikes, the leaves, the sunlight, and the trees we fell for firewood. But we have a pomp-and-circumstance farewell, for Allen is an October child. August, September, and now October. For three months we have moved from celebration to celebration, from hellos to good-byes, and we are ready at the end of October to settle quietly and take our winter rest.

Our baseball season finishes earlier than the official ending, the World Series. For Cubs fans—yes, we admit it—the season nearly always ends too soon. Wait until next year, we cry, but next year produces the same cry as the year before. Despite losing season after season, despite day ball, the Cubs continue to set attendance records. What do the Cubs have that keep people coming to the park? Maybe the fans just love to see the game played, no matter how clumsily. Loyalty, that's what Cubs fans have. There's not much of it left, whether in fans or spouses, employers or employees. We're a flibber-tigibbet society, always ready to switch allegiance at the least adversity. Although there are worse trials than a losing ball club, if a person can't be loyal in a small thing, what will happen when something larger comes along—like fidelity in a marriage or a friendship, or committment to a job? It's all a matter of seeing—seeing where loyalty belongs and why. October is a seeing sort of month, but we foggy-eyed folk have some problems.

Seeing is an art—and a difficult one to learn. Some of Jesus' most poignant miracles came as he gave the gift of sight. We still need it today. We look at trees, rocks, hills, lakes—and people—without seeing them for what they are. Because the days are shorter, the sunlight dimming, we need accute eyesight to see the beauty God puts in front of us. Art students spend years learning to use their eyes, learning to see past the obvious to the planes and structures that undergird creation. We could all benefit from a few such lessons.

When it comes to seeing loyalty or truth or falsehood, we have even more difficulty than we do seeing shapes. It takes a combined discipline of physical and mental eyesight. An architect learns to detect the faleshood in a structure, a sculptor to know the flaw in a piece of marble or wood, and yet use it, nevertheless. We need to learn to detect the falsehood in all the structures of

our lives—relationships, businesses, homes, ourselves—at the same time that we see the truth in each
one. To chip away at the falsehood and bring out the
truth requires keen eyes and steady hands. And practice.
Some days we succeed better than others.

There are days when we just can't seem to get our
eyes open. We bump into things, people, and ideas. No
matter what we try we can't get the hang of what the
day means. We misunderstand what people say. We in-
vent slights and hurts where none were intended. We
misread our mail. Our fingers refuse to type the right
letters and our minds fail to form the proper words. I
call these the original sin days, the days when compromise disappears, chips on shoulders grow, and our
eyes stare inward, hopelessly crossed with the effort.
Although we've got lots of specks in our eyes, we're more
concerned about the beams in everybody else's. Dimly,
we may be aware that our eyes are slightly irritated,
possibly a little bloodshot—but our neighbor's—now
there we see eyes in trouble.

Jesus talked a lot about our eyes. He was conscious
of the proper way of seeing and of how nearsighted we
are. Myopic vision plagues us. If we've seen Jesus, we've
seen the Father, the Bible says; if we had eyes, we'd see
the truth; if we'd clean our eyes, our sight would be
sharper. Most of us ignore the task of keeping our eyes
clean. Isn't that something our tear ducts are for? We
don't think about that any more than we think about
keeping our eyes open.

Yet, our eyes are closed more often than we realize.
Every minute we're awake we blink about twenty-five
times, each blink lasting about a fifth of a second. That
means our eyes are shut five seconds of every minute,
five minutes of every hour, and an hour and a quarter
of every sixteen hours. No wonder we miss so much.

T his is no time to lose an hour and a quarter for every sixteen. There's too much to see—too many leaves, too many pumpkins, too many dying corn stalks—and too much to do to waste our eyesight. The last ball and strike blur into the quarterback's touchdown pass, while the stars come closer than they have since spring. When a friend from Manhattan recently visited us for a marvelous weekend of renewing an old friendship, Allen and I took her fishing at night; her eyes couldn't get enough of the stars. In Manhattan the stars don't exist. Although astronomers tell us that there are many more stars than we can see, I'm grateful for those we can. When I look at them on a clear October evening, I imagine that I am living during the Middle Ages. I do not see space up there, with pinpricks of stars, but a roof, an enclosure, a protection between me and whatever is beyond. Yet, I know that the sky I watch is space, maybe even space expanding, stretching taut like a rubber band or rising yeast. But don't theories of expanding space and Newton's law of gravity seem contradictory?—gravity pulling us down while the universe stretches us.

For me, one of the hazards of shorter days—and yet one of the beauties—is to run at twilight when drivers have trouble seeing me. Twilight is the time when I can watch the emerging stars and think of expanding space and the pull of gravity. Am I growing larger with every second that passes? I imagine it as I run, but the contradiction of the stars, and the reason for running, make it difficult. How can I think of myself stretched like pizza dough at the same time that I'm trying to contain myself? If the theories are right, though, our universe is expanding. Perhaps when space stretches to its greatest extension it will snap back and the sky, as Chicken Little feared, will fall on us.

In the meantime I will continute to imagine myself and my world stretching, growing, expanding, getting ever larger, even though I seem to stay the same size. It's not a bad way to think, because it prevents meanness, pettiness, and other small, niggling irritations from occupying my mind and spirit. This neighbor, that friend, my family are all creatures on the move. We're all bigger than we think; so is our world. But didn't God tell us that a long time ago? Isn't that what the Incarnation is all about?

When we approach our world this way, the smallest, narrowest objects seem to hold the largest thoughts. Nothing is insignificant, neither ants nor antlers. A lunch box day may mean as much as those that are five-starred. Each day in October seems that way to me. So Allen and I follow the example of our squirrels and do our duty. We plow up the garden, sowing field rye, a green manure crop, our way of thanking the earth for abundant vegetables. Carefully, we return the deck furniture to its space in the garage because we want it to last for years. Allen waits for the land to dry and the first hard frost to toughen the ground so that he can begin harvesting trees for firewood. Slowly, irrevocably, the days close in, forcing us to move downstairs.

E ach year we dedicate an October weekend to gathering wood. This is, at the least, a family affair, and often it's a friend affair, too. The growing wood pile calls for a celebration; after hard work comes a succulent and saucy cassoulet, rich, earthy bread, and warm apple pie, made with our own apples. Then, of course, a fire, a story or two—or three—and rest. This is our prelude to Thanksgiving.

It all sounds so simple, so effortless, but our expanding or contracting universe twisted our plans last year. Allen had everything ready. The kids were prepared for their part. A friend stood at chain-saw attention, hard hat in hand. Since they were cutting and splitting wood well back in the woods, Allen planned to use our small tractor and cart to haul out the wood. Two flat tires—one on the tractor, one on the cart—nearly wrecked the day. Because they had already felled a tree when the tires gave out, while Allen and John felled another black walnut, the kids carried, split, and stacked the first one.

A boy who weighs eighty-five pounds can't find it easy to split wood with our monster mauler, a remarkable twelve-pound splitting tool, which with one good blow easily separates a large chunk of wood. The key is in the one good blow. Since I can't even lift the mauler above my head, I doubted that Greg could, either, though he insisted on trying, and ended succeeding. He and his brother even argued over who would split and who would stack. Their Uncle Steven, who hates to split wood, helped one year and was so charmed by our monster mauler that he split wood for hours. No splitting axe, no matter how beautiful its blade, can compete.

On that nearly disastrous day, though, we ended it as planned, perhaps without as much wood hauled and stacked as we would have had with the tractor available, but still a good start for our indoor season. Working together has a greater impact on a family than almost anything else they do together. People who have cut and split wood together, and then watched it burn, have a bond unlike any other. We have some new friends who recently moved to this area. They had heated their former home with wood they had cut; they begged us to let them help us. We would be doing them a favor; "We're suffering from condo-rot," they explained. A lot of us are, and there's no better cure than a day of October work.

The physical and spiritual refreshment that comes from cutting wood is magnified by working under Shakespeare's spell, under his yellow leaves and sear. Some people take color tours in October to capture the magic on film; we are content to stay where we are. We are jealous of our leaves. If our yard may not have the best fall colors, our street does. So does our neighborhood or our drive to work. The trees surrounding the lake where we fish can't be beat. Although we see the same trees every day, we try to notice what we see; we try to make discoveries.

We're always surprised. That particular tree never turned so brilliant a clear yellow, did it? Look how the lake reflects the color of the trees and becomes almost as colorful as the trees themselves. See that fish, just where the shadow of those trees meets the sun? October is a month for seeing. But really its a month for all the senses.

I'm never certain which sense I enjoy the most. Sight and touch affect me greatly, but smell—smell always seems to edge out the others. Of all the senses God gave us, smell is the most direct. Sight, touch, and taste take circuitous routes to the brain; not so with smell, which goes directly to the cerebral cortex, the thinking part of the brain. Before we can form the words, we're aware of the scent of someone burning leaves, woodsmoke from a first fall fire, rotting vegetation in the compost bin, or wool clothes wet from a surprise shower. There's so much to see and smell and taste and touch at this time of year; God is again playing the profligate to no one's greater delight than his.

He wants us in on it. God wants us to notice October, as well as each of his other seasons. Don't be bored, he says; Don't dread the day, don't worry about the routines. My contours are all around you. You can sniff my aroma, hear my rustle. "O taste and see that the Lord is good," wrote the Psalmist. Never mind that he's mixed his metaphors. So has God, for all metaphors meet and become one in him. We could add to the Psalm, O smell and see. O touch and see. O hear and see. O look and see. God, indeed, is good.